READING
Triumphs

Mc Graw Hill **Macmillan McGraw-Hill**

RFB&D
learning through listening

Students with print disabilities may be eligible to obtain an accessible, audio version of the pupil edition of this textbook. Please call Recording for the Blind & Dyslexic at 1-800-221-4792 for complete information.

B

The *McGraw·Hill* Companies

 **Macmillan McGraw-Hill**

Published by Macmillan/McGraw-Hill, of McGraw-Hill Education, a division of
The McGraw-Hill Companies, Inc., Two Penn Plaza, New York, New York 10121.

Printed in the United States of America

ISBN 0-02-192019-2

2 3 4 5 6 7 8 9 071 10 09 08 07 06

CONTENTS

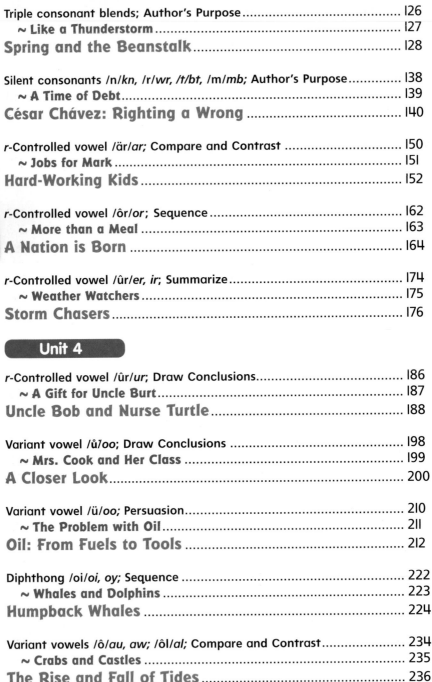

Skills and Strategies

Decoding

Decode these words. What do you notice about the spellings?

miss	tan	hop	pack
bend	ant	bell	sing
fun	tack	job	fill

Vocabulary

hint	gym	news
hunt	odd	

Comprehension

PROBLEM AND SOLUTION In most stories, the characters have a problem. Understanding the problem and how the characters try to solve it can help you understand the story.

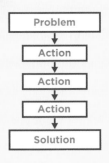

Use your Problem and Solution Chart to figure out the characters' problems.

Read

Look for the problem and solution in the passage.

The Missing Bag

Rick must pack his pants, top, and bat to play ball. But he has lost his gym bag. Rick has to hunt for it.

Rick digs in his closet. There is no gym bag. Rick looks under his bed. There is no bag. This is odd! Where can it be?

Rick runs to ask his mom if she has a hint. Mom smiles. She has good news for Rick. She has his bag!

Fill in the **Problem and Solution Chart** for "The Missing Bag." Use the chart to summarize the passage.

Miss Tan's Hints

by Heather Andrews
illustrated by K. Michael Crawford

The First Task

At ten, the kids went to Miss Tan's class. Miss Tan was not in. Miss Tan had left an odd note about an assignment.

Assignment
This is work, but it is fun.
Get set and learn!
Find hint number one!

Hint
Drums tap and bells ring.
Where does Miss Beck sing?

"Miss Beck sings in the band room!" yelled Max. "Run!"

Jon got the next hint.

Hint
Rocks and sand,
bugs and ants.
Can you find
a class on plants?

"It must be the science room!"
yelled Lin. "Run!"

Rob got the next hint.

Hint
*Look for a cup of jam
and a hot bun.
This job is a mess,
but it is fun!*

"It is about Miss Land!" yelled
Ann. "She cooks us food! Run!"

The Last Hint

A hint sat next to a big pot.

Hint
Jump, hop, run, and bend.
You are almost at the end!

"I bet Miss Tan is in the gym!" yelled Sam. "Run!"

The kids ran into the gym and met Miss Tan.

Tim Mack, with his bat and cap, was there. So was a man from the TV news desk, and a dancer in pink.

A man in a big hat held a cake.
It looked good.

"This is a job hunt!" said the man.

"A job hunt?" asked Lin.

"I left hints about lots of jobs," said
Miss Tan. "I sent you on a job hunt. Hints
helped you think of jobs we can do. Pick
a person and ask about a job."

"I want to help the sick, like Mom can," said Dan.

"Great! And here's a last hint," said Miss Tan. "Always hand in your best work. If you work hard and do not quit, you can get a job you want! It is a fact!"

Comprehension Check

Summarize

Read "Miss Tan's Hints" again. Then summarize the story.

Think About It

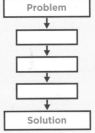

1. Why did Miss Tan send her students on a job hunt?

2. Why did Miss Tan use hints?

3. Which hint was the hardest to figure out? Why do you think so?

4. Think about what Miss Tan said: "If you work hard and do not quit, you can get a job you want!" Do you agree? Why or why not?

Write About It

Think about the jobs that interest you the most. Write down one job and describe how it matches your skills.

Skills and Strategies

Decoding

Decode these words. What do you notice about the spellings?

flat	trip	slip	grand
drink	stem	trunk	stamp
crop	spin	drop	plant

Vocabulary

desert	cactus	dusk
tunnels	shimmer	

Comprehension

MAIN IDEA AND DETAILS The main idea is the most important point of a paragraph or a section. A main idea may be stated or unstated. The details give information that supports the main idea.

Main Ideas	Details

A Main Idea Chart can help you find a main idea and supporting details.

Find the main idea of each paragraph.

The Cactus Plant

A cactus is an amazing plant. It can live in hot desert sand. A cactus has a big green trunk. The cactus drinks water at dusk and stores it in its trunk. The cactus can use the water when the desert is dry.

Cactus can be a home for animals. Birds and bugs live in the trunk. Pack rats dig tunnels under it to make homes. They put things that shimmer on top of the nest.

The cactus plant is the life of the desert.

Make a **Main Idea Chart** for each paragraph. Then use it to help you find the main idea of the passage.

In the Hot Sand

by Nancy Smith

What is a Desert Pack Rat?

Are you a "pack rat"? A pack rat is a person who collects a lot of stuff. But a desert pack rat is an animal. It hunts for stuff for its nest.

A pack rat looks like most rats, but it has a soft tail. It has big ears and big eyes. Its toes are long and thin. A pack rat can be tan, gray, or black. Its fur is quite soft.

A pack rat's big ears can help it sense danger.

A pack rat gets food and water from cactus plants. It uses cactus plants to build its nest. A pack rat can run up the stem of a cactus and not get stuck.

A pack rat has a cactus snack.

Flowering cactus plants grow in the desert.

A pack rat can help a desert. As a pack rat runs on the sand, it drops bits of plants. The bits of plants set roots. This helps new plants grow.

At dusk, the desert cools off.

The Pack Rat's Nest

A pack rat digs its nest at dusk. After sunset, the sun is not as hot. A pack rat digs until its nest has lots of tunnels. One tunnel is for resting. Another is for food.

After a pack rat digs its nest, it gets odd stuff to stack on top. A pack rat likes things that shimmer. It gets shiny keys and tin cans. As it runs home, it may drop a can and pick up a rock.

A pack rat has made a nest in a truck.

A pack rat drops what it finds on top of its nest. Its stack can get big. A pack rat digs new tunnels in its stack. Bugs and lizards can make homes in the stack.

This stack is on top of a pack rat's nest.

Snakes live in the desert, too.

To keep its nest safe, a pack rat puts cactus on top. Its nest is kept safe from foxes and owls. But a snake can slip in. If the pack rat has not run, a snake will eat it.

Pack rats are most active in the desert at night.

   If you see a cactus plant in a desert, look for a pack rat and its nest. Pack rats use plants to live. Pack rats help deserts grow.

Comprehension Check

Summarize

Read "In the Hot Sand"
again. Fill in the Main Idea
Chart as you read. Then use
it to summarize the selection.

Main Ideas	Details

Think About It

1. What do pack rats do to help deserts?

2. How do you think a snake can slip into a pack rat's nest?

3. What things do you collect? Why do you collect them?

4. What other animal do you know of that collects or hides things?

Write About It

People collect things just like pack rats.
Why do you think people like to have
collections?

Skills and Strategies

Decoding

Decode these words. What do you notice about the spellings?

path	whip	trash	with
this	when	dusk	camp
stem	fish	things	nest

Vocabulary

national	trek	raft
fond	canyons	

Comprehension

MAIN IDEA AND DETAILS The main idea is the most important point of a selection. The details give information that supports the main idea. A Main Idea Chart can help you find a main idea and supporting details.

Main Ideas	Details

Find the main idea of the passage.

National Parks

Are you fond of swimming and fishing? You can swim and fish in national parks. Look for parks with water. At some parks, you can take a trip on a raft. Other parks have hills to trek up. You can camp in parks if you wish.

To be safe, never swim alone. Also, you must never feed the animals! If you can go into canyons, stay on paths. Stay in camp after the sun sets. It is not safe to go on paths after dusk.

Make a **Main Idea Chart** for each paragraph. Use the charts to figure out the main idea of the passage.

WHERE SHOULD WE GO?

by Rhonda Ray

NATIONAL PARKS

Trish is helping Phil plan a trip. Phil is her big brother. Phil is fond of hot spots. But he also wants to swim. Where should he go? We can help him hunt for a spot. Maybe he can visit a national park!

In the West, many parks have deep canyons. They have red rocks and hot sand. Only plants like cactus can grow there. Pack rats live there. You can see these things if you trek in a desert.

Some parks have ponds. You can swim if it gets hot. You can take a raft trip. Some ponds have duck nests. It is fun to find a nest with eggs!

Grand Teton National Park, Wyoming

A beach on Cape Cod.

Some parks have water and sand. This is a beach. It is a park, too! You can swim, fish, or rest in the sun. You can dig in wet sand.

PACKING FOR THIS TRIP

Phil can pick from many parks. He will need to bring lots of things. We can help him pack for this big trip.

Send a postcard from a park.

Parks can be hot or cold. But some things are the same for any trip. It is best to bring a hat, socks, pants, and tops. Phil can pack his things in a backpack.

Be prepared for all kinds of weather when you pack.

It is always good to pack a first-aid kit for a camping trip.

Phil must pack special things for this trip. He may wish to camp or swim. He should pack spray to stop bugs. He should bring sun block. He should also pack a clock and a lamp.

At a park, Phil will pick a spot to camp. He can camp in a van or in a tent. He can unpack and hang up his bag. It will help keep his things safe.

A lake in Minnesota.

Parks can be fun. There are many parks to visit. Phil can plan lots of trips. You can read about parks and plan trips, too.

A park sign in Alaska.

Comprehension Check

Summarize

Read "Where Should We Go?"
again. Fill in the Main Idea
Chart as you read. Then use it
to summarize the selection.

Main Ideas	Details

Think About It

1. What things would you take on a trip?
   Explain.

2. Why can you swim in some parks, and
   not in others?

3. Write about a park near your home.

4. Reread page 23 in "In the Hot
   Sand." What animal is mentioned in
   both selections?

Write About It

What can people do to take care of our
national parks? Explain.

Skills and Strategies

Decoding

Decode these words. What do you notice about the spellings?

path	ship	ride	white
this	brave	plane	prize
shade	state	nine	theme

Vocabulary

vanished	pit	chamber
relate	bases	

Comprehension

CHARACTER Stories are about people, or characters. Understanding characters can help you better understand a story.

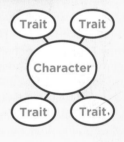

A Character Web helps you figure out a character's traits, or personality.

Identify the character and character traits.

Pete's Dream

Pete likes the moon. His mom let him put moon posters on his walls. Pete vanished one night at dusk. His mom spotted him watching the moon.

Pete got a prize for a tale contest. He had to relate his space ideas. Pete made up the best tale. His prize was a trip to Space Camp.

Pete plans to ride up to space when he gets big. He will live on a moon base. He will have his own chamber. He plans to write a tale about an odd pit on the moon.

Fill in the **Character Web** for "Pete's Dream." Then use it to help you summarize the passage.

Kate in Space

by Joan Smith
illustrated by Tom Leonard

Take a Trip to The Moon

Kate sent in a page to the national Space Ride Contest. Kate filled her page with facts about her life. These facts tracked Kate's love of space. Pete Chase, of Space Ride, called Kate to tell her that she had won!

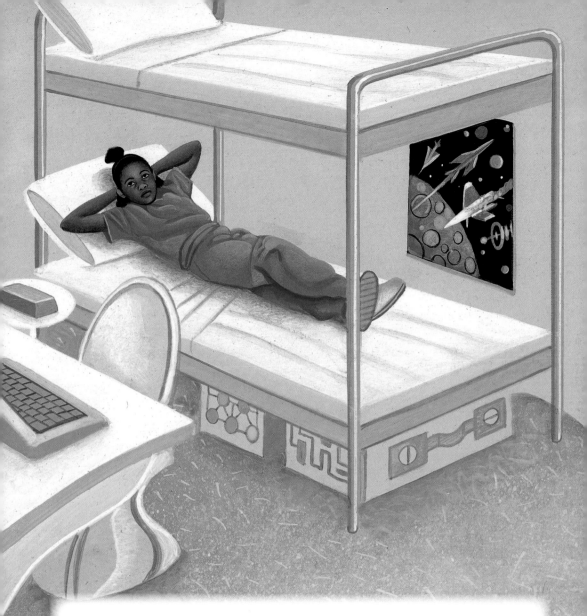

   Kate's prize was a trip to the moon!
Take-off was at ten!

   Kate felt brave for taking a ride in space.
Kate did not stop thinking about this trip.
What did Earth look like from space? Kate
could not wait!

Kate, Mom, and Dad had to ride a
plane to a space ship named GATE3. The
trip took a long time.

GATE3 landed at dusk. The moon had
lots of rocks, hills, and canyons. Kate saw
a lot of white huts. These white huts were
space bases.

Kate, Mom, and Dad wanted to rest when they got to Space Base Nine. Kate unpacked her bag. Mom, Dad, and Kate were shocked that the food tasted fresh. They filled their plates and ate and ate. They went to bed quite late.

The next day, Kate, Mom, and Dad put
on space tops and pants. The tops and
pants kept them safe from cold shade and
hot sun.

Lost in Space

When they left Space Base Nine, Kate, Mom, and Dad did not just step out. Mom had to unlock the glass door. It went into a chamber. Dad flipped a big lock to trap air in Space Base Nine. Then it was safe to get out.

Mom, Dad, and Kate had a ride in a space truck. Kate wanted to hunt for space rocks. She heard that this side of the moon had shining rocks. Kate spotted a pile of rocks. Kate jumped out of the truck and ran to grab a rock.

Then Kate vanished! Mom and Dad did not stop to think. They ran to find Kate.

Mom and Dad saw a lamp shining from a pit. Kate had slipped and fallen in! Mom and Dad helped Kate get back out.

Mom and Dad felt glad that Kate was safe. Back at the base, Mom said that Kate must not run off on her own. Kate said that was a wise plan. But Kate could not wait to relate this tale to her pals back on Earth!

Comprehension Check

Summarize

Read "Kate in Space" again. Then summarize the story.

Think About It

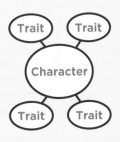

1. Kate jumped out of the truck and ran to grab a rock. Fill in your web with a word that describes Kate.

2. Do you think Kate was a little worried about traveling to the moon? Why?

3. If you could live on the moon, would you want to? Explain.

4. Tell about how Space Base Nine and your home are alike and different.

Write About It

Do you think it might be wise for people to live on the moon someday? Explain.

Skills and Strategies

Decoding

Decode these words. What do you notice about the spellings?

pole	huge	wake	home
drove	tune	bone	whales
dove	ride	stole	hope

Vocabulary

peered   pride   dove

fins   locate overflowing

Comprehension

CHARACTER, SETTING, PLOT Knowing the setting can help you figure out why events occur and why characters act the way they do.

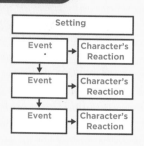

A Setting Flow Chart can help you understand the story.

Identify the character, setting and plot.

June Hopes for Whales

Mom, Dad, and June drove to the beach for a swim. June peered into the waves. She hoped to locate whales. Mom and Dad watched with pride as June swam and dove.

Dad rubbed his toes in the wet sand. Mom swam on her back and got hot.

Mom and Dad came back to sit in the sun. Then June saw a whale. It had big fins. June waved to the whale and yelled, "Hello." She was overflowing with joy.

Fill in the **Setting Flow Chart** for "June Hopes for Whales." Then use it to summarize the passage.

At Home with Whales

by John Archer

illustrated by Lina Chesak

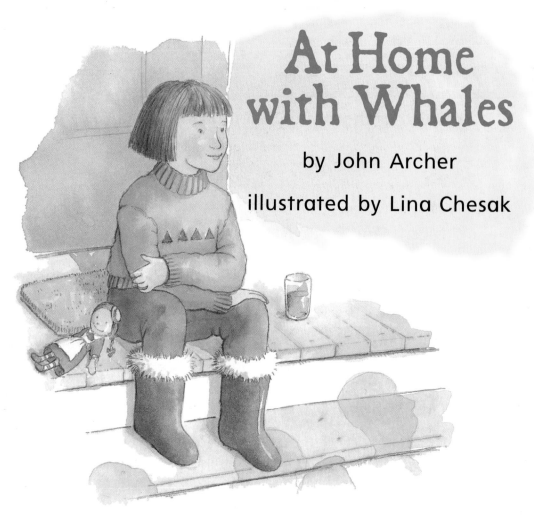

June on the Job

June woke up at six. She sat at the side of her home and faced the sea. June liked the waves.

June's dad led whale trips. He took people out to see whales. June helped him.

June went in to wake Dad up.

"We must get to the boat, June," Dad said. "People like to get spots to stand. Don't forget to grab some ham and eggs. You have quite a job today!"

"I did not think I had time to eat!" smiled June.

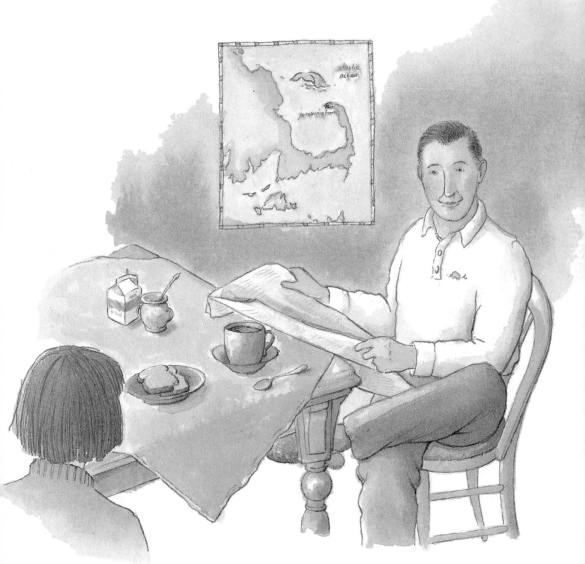

June's dad led the quick trek to the dock. It was overflowing with people. Some hoped to see birds and sea life. But most hoped to see humpback whales!

June gave out life vests and maps.

Cole, his dad, and his stepmom came on this trip. Cole gave June a wide smile.

"It is time to set off on our five-mile ride!" June said with pride.

Cole and the Whales

June's boat was a mile out to sea.

"Will we see a whale?" Cole asked June.

"I hope we see humpback whales," said June. "Dad can locate them. One time I saw nine!"

"Your dad must be wise about humpback whales," Cole said.

Just then, June saw fins rise up from the water. "Look at the whales!"

Cole and June watched the whales wave their huge fins. Cole had quite a tale to relate when he got home.

"Listen!" yelled June.

Cole peered at the water. He heard a crashing sound as the whales smacked the water with their fins.

"Dad says whales talk like that," June said.

"I like these whales!" Cole said.

One whale swam up next to the boat.
It was about 40 feet long. It swam on its
side and waved its fin. The people smiled
and clapped.

The whales jumped up and then dove
back in at the same time. Then the whales
chased each other. It was fun to see
humpback whales jumping and playing!
The humpback whales gave Cole and
June the trip of a lifetime, then vanished.

Comprehension Check

Summarize

Read "At Home with Whales" again. Then summarize the story.

Think About It

1. What did one whale do? How did the people react?

2. What other animals might June and Cole have seen from the boat?

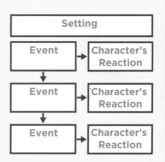

3. What animal would you really like to see, and why?

4. Reread p. 52 of "Kate in Space." How is Cole's experience similar to Kate's?

Write About It

June's dad's ship was very full. Why do you think so many people are interested in watching wildlife? Explain.

Skills and Strategies

Decoding

Decode these words. What do you notice about the spellings?

play	tone	fail	home
gray	train	clay	game
snail	stayed	rule	plain

Vocabulary

rude	fame	spite
secured	arranged	

Comprehension

AUTHOR'S PURPOSE Authors write for three reasons: to entertain, inform, or persuade. They may write to make you happy or sad (to entertain), to give you facts (to inform), or to make you believe something (to persuade).

Clue	Clue	Clue

↓ ↓ ↓

Author's Purpose

Use your Author's Purpose Map to find clues to the author's purpose.

Look for the author's purpose.

Play Ball

Baseball is a game that is arranged for two teams. Teams take turns hitting the ball.

When players get hits, they run around the bases. If a player hits a home run, the team has secured a point.

If players win many games, they may also find fame! Sometimes, losing teams can be rude out of spite. But both teams always hope for the best game.

Fill in the **Author's Purpose Map** for "Play Ball." Use the map to summarize the passage.

Gail At the Game

by Madison Jones

illustrated by Dom Lee

When I was nine, Dad went away. A lot of men did. It was 1942, and there was a big war.

Mom and I stayed at home. I sent notes to Dad. I liked to tell him about classes and about our gray cat, Snail.

Playing Baseball

A lot of what I sent Dad was about baseball. Dad had helped train me when he was at home.

The boys in my class were rude. Ray and Duke said "Gail, girls cannot play baseball! Get lost!" But I still played at home until Dad left.

Then Mom and I went on a trip to a big park. It had a field with grass. I did not believe it.

"This is a baseball game," I said. "But there are no men left to play!"

"Take a close look at the players," said Mom.

I peered at the field, and had a shock! They had long hair and dresses! Then Mom explained things.

When war came, male players went away just as Dad had. But people still wished to see games. Women wished to play. A man arranged games with just women.

Can Women Play?

Mom told me that just the best players got picked. They played games in many places. They had to play in dresses. But the dresses made it hard to play. Players secured them back to keep them out of the way.

The first games did not go well.
Those who came poked fun at the players.
They did not think women could play.

"In spite of rude people, the women played with pride," Mom said. "People liked these games."

I liked them, too! The women batted
and ran bases as well as men. One player hit
a home run! I wished Ray and Duke
could see this game!

When the men came home in 1945, they went back to playing baseball. Women kept playing, but things changed. People wished to see games with male players.

After nine years, the women's games ended. I wish I could have played with them.

These women players made the Hall of Fame. They showed that women can play as well as men. They made a path for women players. Today girls and boys can play games like baseball together!

Comprehension Check

Summarize

Read "Gail at the Game" again. Then summarize the story.

Think About It

1. What does the author want you to know about the game of baseball?

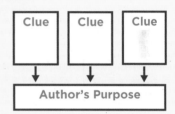

2. How did the women's baseball teams lead the way for female athletes?

3. What sport or activity do you like to do?

4. What other things do you think women may have done to help out?

Write About It

Why do you think baseball is so popular?
What other sports do people watch?

Skills and Strategies

Decoding

Decode these words. What do you notice about the spellings?

neat	lean	tray	sweet
easy	paint	beans	green
treat	deep	main	feels

Vocabulary

cheap	gulf	steamboat
frame	feast	

Comprehension

MAKE INFERENCES Sometimes an author makes a point that is not directly stated in the story. You can use

Text Clues	What you Know	Inferences

clues to decide what the author means. This will help you understand the story.

Use an Inferences chart to figure out the author's meaning.

Look for the inferences.

The Gulf and Me

We live next to a gulf. There are many green trees here. I see lots of birds' nests. I watch the birds feast on fish.

I see passing steamboats, as well. They please me so much that I make toy steamboats when I have time.

I have a kit to help me make them. These kits are cheap, so I can have more than one. I need help making the boat frames. I like the gulf. I hope we stay here!

Fill in the **Inferences Word Web** for "The Gulf and Me." Use the web to retell the passage.

79

A Year in My Life

by Joyce Mayberry
illustrated by John Trotta

Leaving Home

April 15, 1839

My name is Bea, and I am nine. Granddad gave me this diary to make notes in. We will leave our home in Kentucky and go to Texas. There is a lot of cheap land in Texas. We will set up a farm there.

April 18, 1839

My brother Reed is ten. His best friend Gabe gave him a rock as a gift. I gave my bed to my best friend, Wendy. We can't take it with us. I hope that she has lots of sweet dreams in it.

May 2, 1839

We traded our home for a wagon and mules. A wagon is just like a home that moves. Granddad made us ham and beans at home before we left.

We rode a whole day and stopped and slept when the sun set.

May 8, 1839

Today we put our wagon and mules on a steamboat. It was on its way to New Orleans. The boat was huge and white. It had a big wheel on its side. The wheel made it go.

May 21, 1839

We stayed in a big home
in New Orleans for a time.
We met the Keans. They became
our new friends. Reed and
I went on a long walk with
the Keans. Then we had tea.

New Places to see

June 1, 1839

We left New Orleans last week. We rode on a sailing ship across the gulf. The water was deep. Gulls dove in to get fish.

We just got to Texas. People feel that Texas will become a state! I think it will be fun to live here.

June 15, 1839

We have our own land at last.
It has a creek over the hill! I will
wade in it. Reed will help cut logs
for a new home. A frame must be put
up first. Then we will all plant corn
and beans.

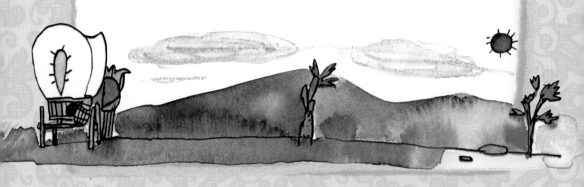

October 2, 1839

Our home is finished. We had a feast with friends. The beans tasted just fine. And we had fish from the creek.

A nice lady up the creek will help us with Spanish. A lot of people speak it here.

Our friends, the Keans, will get here later. They will live close to us.

April 15, 1840

This has been a good year, in spite of the move. Texas isn't a strange place now. It feels like home. Reed and I are Spanish speakers now. A greeting I like to use is "hola."

This is the last page. I will keep this diary and read it to my children with pride.

Comprehension Check

Summarize

Read "A Year in My Life" again. Then summarize the story.

Think About It

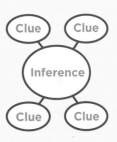

1. How does Bea feel about the move? Use details from the story to fill in your chart.

2. Why did Bea's family leave Kentucky?

3. Have you ever moved to a new place or helped a new kid at school? What did you learn?

4. Bea learns Spanish in Texas. What else will Bea learn in her new home?

Write About It

Bea is excited about life in a new place. What are some things people can look forward to when they move?

Skills and Strategies

Decoding

Decode these words. What do you notice about the spellings?

high	spy	cry	flight
really	fry	beet	sign
grind	tiny	find	sight

Vocabulary

protected	soar	various
festival	eager	dazzling

Comprehension

FACT AND OPINION A fact is something that can be proven to be true. An opinion is based on someone's feelings.

Fact	Opinion

A Fact and Opinion Chart can help you find facts and opinions.

Look for the facts and opinions.

A Chinese Pal

My best pal is Chinese. I like to go to his home. We drink tea and he tells me various things about China. Giant pandas live in China. They are protected so that they live a long time.

He likes flying kites. Kites can have dazzling colors. He gave me a painting of a kite that soars high in the sky.

There are festivals in China. They seem like fun! He likes it here, but he is eager to go back soon.

Make a **Fact and Opinion Chart** for "A Chinese Pal." Use the chart to figure out whether statements are facts or opinions.

Up in the Sky

By Yin Hsu

Take a trip up a hill on a windy day. What is flying high in the skies? It isn't a bird or a plane. It is a kite!

Kids and grown-ups like flying kites. Long ago, the first kites were made by people in China. Then, people around the world began flying kites.

Kite-flying in Japan, 1860s

One tale claims a man's hat got lifted off by wind. He had fun chasing it, so he did it again! His hat became the first kite.

Other tales say that people liked watching leaves on windy days. They tied leaves to strings and watched them fly.

93

English kite, 1903

Long ago, kites became important in keeping China protected. A man might be lifted up by a kite while he spied on an enemy. He could use the kite to soar high like a plane. He could also fight from the air!

Chinese kites blowing in the wind

Kites are used for many things. They come in various shapes and sizes.

Kites can be cloth or paper. In China, most kites are made of silk secured by bamboo frames. Kites can be painted with dazzling colors. A kite might be shaped like a dragon, a fish, or just a plain box.

This fisherman holds a kite made from a leaf.

Types of Kites

You can use a kite to catch fish. First you tie a fishing line to a kite. Then you put bait on the line. You watch the kite eagerly as it flies over the water. When you tug the kite down, you might find a fish on your line! Some people think this is more fun than using a fishing pole.

If you have something to say, try using a kite! Kites can send messages in the sky. A kite may tell of a new baby or a wedding.

A kite can be used to wish you luck. The Japanese fly kites at the New Year. They make kites with lucky signs.

A kite from Korea

Many countries set up special days to honor kites. You can see kites fly. People make and sell many types of kites. In Italy, they make whale kites with white eyes on black cloth.

A whale kite flies on the beach.

Colorful kites brighten up the sky.

China has a Kite Day festival on September ninth. People make and fly grand kites. They feast on snacks and spend all day flying kites.

You might see famous fighter kites. People fly these kites quite fast and try to cut another flyer's line.

A worker paints kites at a workshop in China

There is much to learn about kites. From long ago in China until now, kites have had many uses. They have been used for fighting, spying, and fishing. But the best way to use a kite is to fly it high for fun!

Comprehension Check

Summarize

Read "Up In The Sky" again. Then retell the story.

Think About It

1. List three facts and opinions about kites. Use them to fill in your chart.

Fact	Opinion

2. Why were kites so important to the Chinese?

3. If you could design a kite, what would it look like? Explain.

4. Kites are used for many things. What could you use a kite for?

Write About It

Many countries set up special days to honor events or people. Describe something you would like to honor.

Skills and Strategies

Decoding

Decode these words. What do you notice about the vowel spellings?

glow	most	light	goal
bold	final	coal	known
fly	flows	nobody	groan

Vocabulary

experiments	electric	provided
invention	improve	operated

Comprehension

PROBLEM AND SOLUTION In most stories, the characters have a problem. Understanding how the characters try to solve the problem helps you understand the story.

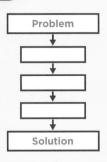

Use your Problem and Solution Chart to figure out the characters' problems.

Look for the problem and solution.

On the Road with Henry

Henry Ford had a goal. He wanted to improve things. One day, he spotted a horseless buggy. This provided him with a bold plan.

He wanted to make a car that operated on gas alone. He did many experiments. Today he is known by most people for this invention.

Later in life, Ford met Thomas Edison. He also made life easier. He invented an electric light that glows in the dark!

Fill out the **Problem and Solution** Chart for "On the Road with Henry." Use the chart to retell the passage.

Edison Shows the Way

by Carla Fitzgerald

illustrations by Steve Cieslawski

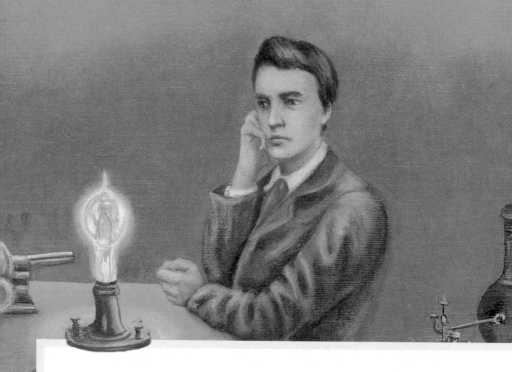

What Glows in the Dark?

We need light for most things these days. We need light to work and play. We need power to make lights glow. But 150 years ago, no one had power for lights!

Thomas Edison liked inventing things. As a kid, he asked lots of questions. His teachers didn't like this. But his mom knew why he asked. He wished to know about things.

Thomas Edison as a young boy in the 1850s

Edison studied at home until he was 12. Then he got a job on the railroad. He sold newspapers. He used his pay to get various things for his experiments. He set up a lab on the train. He did experiments in between sales.

Then he got a job running a telegraph. It was a machine that sent messages. It used sound to spell words. Edison liked this machine, and he liked the job.

Edison was eager to help people. This led him to invent new things. He also tried to improve things. He made the telephone better. But he did not stop there.

Seeing the Light

Edison set up a big factory. He got people to help with his inventions. He made and sold most of them. He invented more than a thousand things! All of them came in handy.

Edison's phonograph, made in 1878

One big thing he made was the phonograph. This later became the record player. It recorded sounds on a tube wrapped in tin, which was set on a frame. Then it played these sounds back. It was not like a tape deck or CD player. But the phonograph was a hit in Edison's time.

The most famous thing he made was the light bulb. Long ago, people used gas lamps. Edison made a light bulb that operated on electricity. He set up electrical plants and lines. This provided light for a lot of people.

First Edison electric lighting station, New York City, 1882

Thomas Edison invented and fixed many things. He helped people to lead better lives. Think of him when you see light bulbs glowing!

Thomas Edison shows his first electric light.

Comprehension Check

Summarize

Read "Edison Shows the Way" again. Then summarize the selection.

Think About It

1. What made Edison want to invent and improve things? Use details from the selection to fill in your chart.

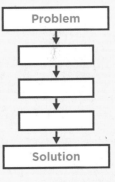

2. How did the invention of the light bulb help people?

3. Tell about an invention that is important to you.

4. Why did Edison's teachers think asking lots of questions was a bad trait?

Write About It

What do you think is the most important thing Edison invented or improved?

Skills and Strategies

Decoding

Decode these words. What do you notice about the spellings?

lunch	check	reach	chase
chill	patch	chest	bench
watch	crunchy	teacher	ranch

Vocabulary

clutched   escape   rattle

nervous   poison

Comprehension

MAKE INFERENCES Sometimes an author makes a point that is not directly stated in the story. You can use clues

Text Clues	What you Know	Inferences

to decide what the author means. This will help you understand the story.

Use an Inferences chart to figure out the author's meaning.

Look for the inferences.

Watching Snakes

Joe watches TV shows about snakes. He knows which snakes have poison and which do not.

In one show, a man found a snake on a ranch. He clutched it gently by its head. It began to rattle its tail!

The man was not nervous. The snake could not bite him or escape. Joe would like to have a snake as a pet one day.

Fill in the **Inferences Word Web** for "Watching Snakes." Use the web to retell the passage.

The Snake Watcher

by Joan Mitchell
illustrated by Laura Bryant

"Wait!" yelled Ana. She and her sister Inez were taking a bike ride. Ana had stopped to pick up a rattlesnake rattle in a patch of sagebrush. Inez did not see that Ana was not matching her speed.

"Ana, you must ride close to me!" Inez shouted. "You might fall off!"

Ana's Big Find

Ana stopped her bike next to Inez in front of the shop.

She tried to show Inez what she had picked up. But Inez was just thinking about lunch.

Inez and Ana saw their neighbors.
Mr. Branch spotted the rattle clutched in
Ana's hand. He remembered that she knew
a lot about snakes.

"Hi, Ana," said Mr. Branch. "Do you
have time to teach my kids about snakes?
I will get a newspaper. It will not take me
much time."

The kids sat on a bench. Chad and his sister Rachel leaned in to see the rattle in Ana's hand. They seemed a bit nervous.

Ana opened her mouth wide. She pretended to bite the kids like a snake. "Just kidding," she grinned. "Snakes don't often bite people. Let me tell you about them."

Shy and Scary Snakes

"I used to be scared of snakes. But now I think snakes are neat," Ana said.

Ana went on, "Did you know that poison is a trait of some snakes, such as the rattlesnake? It tells us to stay away by shaking its rattle. This gives us time to escape."

Ana showed the kids how the sidewinder rattlesnake slides.

"It moves sideways. Just its head and tail reach the sand. It slides over and over." Ana smiled. "This slide leaves s-shaped tracks in the sand."

"That is funny," said Chad. "I'd like to see a sidewinder."

"We saw a pretty snake with red, yellow, and black bands on it. It was at the ranch," said Rachel.

"Oh, you must have seen a coral snake," Ana said. "We don't see much of them. They are not eager to be seen."

The kids grinned. They felt glad that coral snakes were shy!

"There is a snake that has dazzling blue and black skin. It is an indigo snake. It can grow as long as eight feet! But it has no poison," added Ana.

"Thanks for teaching us about snakes," said Rachel.

"I will check the web. It might provide more facts on snakes!" said Chad.

"Glad to help," said Ana, shaking the rattle in her hand. "Snakes are fun to watch, but don't try to catch them! They are not harmless!"

Inez checked her watch. It was time to go home for lunch. Ana and Inez ran back to their bikes. They waved good-bye.

Comprehension Check

Summarize

Read "The Snake Watcher" again. Then summarize the story.

Think About It

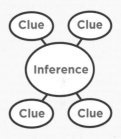

1. How did Chad and Rachel feel about snakes at the beginning of the story?

2. Why does Ana know about snakes?

3. Think about other animals that people fear. Do you think people should fear these animals? Explain.

4. Reread page 105 of "Edison Shows the Way." How is Edison similar to Ana?

Write About It

Why do people need to learn about snakes? What can people do to be more comfortable around snakes? Explain.

Skills and Strategies

Decoding

Decode these words. What do you notice about the spellings?

scrape	sprint	screamed	strum
spring	strap	streaming	screen
spray	street	splash	strong

Vocabulary

strolled	sprinted	strained
scruffy	thunderstorm	

Comprehension

AUTHOR'S PURPOSE Authors have reasons for writing. They may write to give you facts, or to make you feel happy or sad. Knowing the author's purpose can help you understand the story.

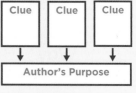

Use your Author's Purpose Map to find clues to the author's purpose.

Look for the author's purpose.

Like a Thunderstorm

Many fairy tales make giants seem mean and scruffy. They are as big as skyscrapers. Most giants make more noise than a thunderstorm!

In one tale, a kid named Jack climbed a beanstalk and met a giant. The giant tried to grab Jack, but Jack got away. He took the giant's treasure.

Jack sprinted back to the beanstalk. The giant strained to catch up! Jack escaped and strolled home. He lived happily ever after!

Fill in the **Author's Purpose Map** for "Like a Thunderstorm." Use the map to summarize the passage.

Spring and the Beanstalk

by Ed Mathis
illustrated by Selina Alko

Spring went to see Dad in his lab. He was studying seeds. "Hi, Dad," said Spring. "What experiment are you working on?"

"I'm growing a beanstalk," said Dad.

"Is it like the one in *Jack and the Beanstalk?*" asked Spring.

"Yes," said Dad. "It's right outside."

Spring strolled into the garden and looked at Dad's huge beanstalk. She felt it would be splendid to reach the top. She stepped onto the plant. Suddenly she was lifted with it up into the sky!

Spring strained to escape, but a deep voice yelled, "I'm Strom the Giant! Stay still!"

The scruffy giant placed Spring in his hand. At first, she was scared. But when Strom smiled, he didn't seem so scruffy.

"What do you want?" Spring asked.

"Our sun is dying!" the giant said. "We need to find a new one!"

"How can I help you find a new sun?" asked Spring.

"Your dad wears a white coat and works in a lab. He must know about this mystery. We need his help!" said Strom.

"Dad doesn't know about mysteries! He's a scientist!" yelled Spring.

"What does that mean?" asked Strom.

"He knows how things work," Spring said.

"Then please get him to help," sniffed Strom. Big tears splashed into his hand.

"Don't cry! I'm getting sprayed," groaned Spring.

Strom put Spring back in the grass. Spring sprinted off to find dad.

Spring Finds an Answer

"Dad! I met Strom, the giant!" cried Spring, running into the lab.

"Did he hurt you?" asked Dad.

"Dad, Strom is not bad. He just needs help. His sun is dying," said Spring.

Dad said, "Maybe we can help him."

Dad clutched Spring's hand as they ran. Then Spring stopped and looked up. She felt that Strom was right about his sun. But her sun must be dying, too! The sky was a deep blue, and the wind felt chilly. Spring felt hopeless. She wished Dad could help.

They found Strom. "The sky is very dark," Strom told Dad. "The sun must be close to dying."

Spring looked at the sky. She saw a flash of lightning and heard a crash of thunder.

"The sun isn't dying! A thunderstorm is on its way!" Spring yelled.

When the rain ended, the sun shined brightly. Strom was happy. Spring and Dad went home.

Dad said, "I think I will grow a crop of beanstalks each spring."

Spring said, "I can use them to visit Strom." She smiled. "He might need our help again!"

Comprehension Check

Summarize

Read "Spring and the Beanstalk" again.
Then summarize the story.

Think About It

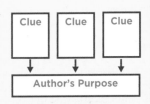

1. Spring says her father is a
   scientist. Why do you think
   the author included this information?

2. Why did Spring think a thunderstorm was
   on the way?

3. Would you enjoy having Spring as a
   friend? Why or why not?

4. Could Dad and Spring have helped Strom
   if the sun really was dying? Explain.

Write About It

Spring helped someone by thinking about
his problem, and figuring out what was
wrong. What can you learn from Spring?

Skills and Strategies

Decoding

Decode these words. What do you notice about the spellings?

knob	limb	wreck	debt
wring	knock	climb	known
wrong	thumb	kneel	wrote

Vocabulary

debt	allow	conditions
attend	roamed	permanent

Comprehension

AUTHOR'S PURPOSE Does the author use fact or humor to get the point across? Facts suggest an author wants to inform. Humor suggests an author wants to entertain.

Clue	Clue	Clue
↓	↓	↓

Author's Purpose

An Author's Purpose Map can help you find the author's purpose.

Look for the author's purpose.

A Time of Debt

In the 1930s, many fell into debt. People roamed the country to find work. Many became farm hands.

Being a farm hand did not allow for much free time. Most farm hands could not get permanent homes. Often, kids of farm hands could not attend classes.

Many knew that things were wrong with the job conditions. They worked together to try to make things better.

Fill in the **Author's Purpose Map** for "A Time of Debt." Use the map to retell the passage.

César Chávez:
Righting a Wrong

by Jenny Pittman

PICKING CROPS

Picking crops is hard work. Farm hands know how to follow the crops. They may start with peaches, then move on to pick peas, apples, and potatoes. They keep moving to find crops that need picking. It is not an easy life. This was the life of César Chávez.

César's grandfather hoped to find a better life. So he left Mexico and came to the United States. He had a farm and raised his children there. César's father owned a shop. He did well, but then the family fell into debt. They lost their home.

Main street of an Oklahoma town, 1938

Farm hands loading carrots onto a truck

In 1937, jobs were not easy to find. César and his family went west to California. They became farm hands. They roamed across the state picking crops. Life was quite strained. They got little pay and had no permanent homes.

The children of farm hands had a hard time. People did not always make them feel at home. It was not easy to go to classes.

César and his brothers and sisters switched schools many times. But César was able to attend classes up to eighth grade.

Kids at school in 1937

Farm hands lining up to get jobs

César felt that farm hands must have better lives. He spoke with the farm owners about pay raises and better conditions. Most farm hands were nervous about what might happen if they helped César. They did not wish to lose their jobs. César made a strong stand. He would fight by himself to improve unfair conditions.

HELPING FARM HANDS

In 1948, he married Helen Fabela. He and his wife knew that farm hands needed to be united. Being united would allow them to fight for better conditions. César and Helen helped farm hands set up a group to fight boldly for their rights.

César Chávez and his wife Helen marching in California

César went to speak with farmers. He knew there were still a lot of things wrong with this job. He got 300 farm hands to join his group. Today this group is known as the United Farm Workers of America.

United Farm Workers of America at a rally

César Chávez leading the fight for workers' rights

In 1965, César helped a group of grape pickers. They wanted better conditions. César told the grape pickers to stop work until they got what they needed. This was called a strike.

A lot of people came to help with the strike. At last, grape growers felt it was time to fix bad farm conditions.

César Chávez speaking at a workers' rally

César kept fighting for the rights of farm hands. He kept them united. He led strikes, wrote, and helped a lot of farm hands escape from a bad life.

César Chávez died in 1993. He was well-known and well-loved. To this day, César's kids keep fighting for the rights of farm hands.

Comprehension Check

Summarize

Read "César Chávez: Righting a Wrong" again. Then summarize the selection.

Think About It

1. What did the author want you to know about César Chávez? Use details to fill in your chart.

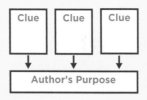

2. Why was it important for farm hands to unite?

3. Describe jobs you do to help at home.

4. What are some ways people are treated unfairly? How could you help?

Write About It

Why do people today move to other places? Explain.

Skills and Strategies

Decoding

Decode these words. What do you notice about the spellings?

knowing	hard	market	garden
farms	wrote	army	thumb
artist	part	target	cards

Vocabulary

advisers	theater	accepted
completed	activities	duty

Comprehension

COMPARE AND CONTRAST

Comparing is telling how things or people are alike. Contrasting is telling how they are different.

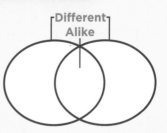

A Venn Diagram shows what is alike and what is different.

Compare and contrast Mark's jobs.

Jobs for Mark

Mark's favorite activities were acting and singing. He got a summer job at the theater.

Mark's job was to sell tickets. When Mark completed his work, he watched the show. The theater's advisers taught him about acting.

When school started, Mark missed his summer job. But he accepted his new job. He goes to school. It is his duty to study hard!

Fill in the **Venn Diagram** for "Jobs for Mark." Use the diagram to retell the passage.

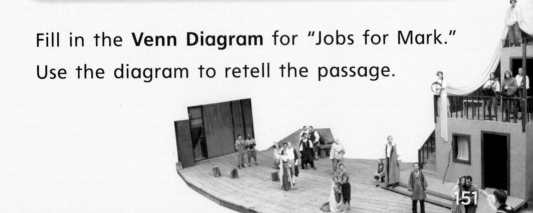

151

Hard-Working Kids

by Mark Collins

A Hard Past

Being a kid is hard! You have to attend class, study, and wash the dishes. And you do all kinds of other activities. You are not alone. Kids have had jobs for ages. Let's read about some of the things kids can do!

Wall painting of King Tut

Kids rule! Well, King Tut did. He lived in Egypt a long time ago. King Tut became king when he was only nine. Being king is a hard job. King Tut had advisers to help him. King Tut did not get to rule long, but he made his mark on history.

Bronze figure of a girl running, 6th century Greece

It is good to be fit, but the kids in Sparta had to be in top shape. Sparta was a city in Greece long ago.

In Sparta, kids sprinted and played athletic games. All males had a duty to join the army. Conditions were tough, but kids in Sparta did the job well.

Have you ever had a part in a class play? If so, you might be interested in this. Hundreds of years ago in England, acting was a job for boys. Sometimes, they acted in street shows. Other times, they got to be on bigger stages, like the Globe theater in London.

An open-air theater in California

American poet Phillis Wheatley writing with a quill pen

Do you like to write? Phillis Wheatley was America's first black poet.

She came to Boston from Africa in 1761. She was an enslaved person in John Wheatley's home. Soon Phillis was welcomed as a member of the family.

She learned English fast and started writing poetry. Her first poem was published at the age of 14. Later, Phillis was accepted as a well-known poet.

From Farms to Fun

As long as there have been farms, kids have had to help. When people settled out west, they had to start new lives. They had to plant crops and make new homes. Even in the wild West, kids completed the job!

Girl feeding chickens in Montana, 1910

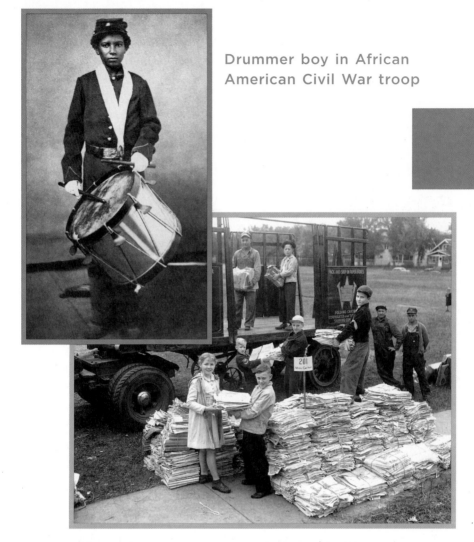

Drummer boy in African American Civil War troop

Kids collect newspapers during World War II.

Kids help out in hard times. In the Civil War, boys became drummers. In World War II, kids helped by planting gardens. Gardens gave people extra food, so more could be sent to the soldiers. Kids also collected newspapers and books to send to fighting men and women.

Today, most kids don't rule countries. But there are lots of things that kids can do. Some kids like playing games, like tennis or baseball. These things take a lot of time and practice.

Other kids like painting, acting, writing, and art. They might take extra classes to improve their skills.

Boy plants flowers for Earth Day in California.

Kids find many ways to enjoy life and help others. Kids can help by cleaning up a park or making cards for sick kids. They might decide to start a magazine for stories, poems, and art. They might start a special club. Kids can do the greatest things when they try!

Comprehension Check

Summarize

Read "Hard-Working Kids" again. Then summarize the selection.

Think About It

1. Compare and contrast two kids from "Hard-Working Kids." Use details to fill in your chart.

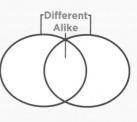

2. Why was it important for kids to help out during war?

3. Tell about activities, chores, or jobs you do.

4. How was César Chávez's early life different from the life of King Tut?

Write About It

What job would you want to have when you grow up? Explain your answer.

Skills and Strategies

Decoding

Decode these words. What do you notice about the spellings?

more	corn	born	march
morning	far	before	storm
sore	starving	acorns	shore

Vocabulary

starving	staff	declared
fetch	distressed	rich

Comprehension

SEQUENCE Sequence is the order in which events in a story take place. Understanding sequence helps you understand the story.

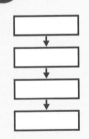

Figure out the most important events in sequence. Use your Sequence Chart to help you.

Look for the sequence of events.

More than a Meal

Long ago, buffalo was a food source for many Native Americans. As long as they had buffalo, they would not starve or be distressed.

When the time to hunt buffalo was declared, hunters fetched their horses. A leader would grab a staff. The hunt would begin.

Buffalo skins made good clothing, and the meat made a rich meal. But the buffalo was more than a meal for Native Americans. It gave them life.

Fill in the **Sequence Chart** for "More than a Meal." Then use it to summarize the passage.

A Nation is Born

as told by Annie Samuels
illustrated by Constance Bergum

More to Eat

Long ago, some people were starving and distressed. They had to roam to hunt deer and pick acorns. But they never had much, and they had to divide it up.

A wise leader felt it was his duty to find more food for his people.

"We need to find a permanent home where we can grow our own crops," he stated. "Then we will not starve."

But where might the people grow their crops? The leader stuck a staff in a pile of stones.

"We will let this staff decide our path," he declared.

The people packed their things and started marching. Each night, the leader stuck his staff in a pile of stones. Each morning, the staff leaned toward the sun.

"We must keep going," the leader said.

The people kept marching. Most had sore feet and legs, and did not want to keep marching. Still, they followed their leader.

The trip was so long that the people cried. They did not think the march would end. Most people carried poles for new homes on their backs. The poles got heavier each day.

The leader put his staff in a pile of stones each night. Each morning the stick leaned toward the sun. So they kept marching.

The Corn Plant

One night, the people came to the shore of a wide creek. The leader stuck his staff in a pile of stones. The next morning the staff leaned toward the creek. So the people made rafts and rode across the creek. They felt happy that they didn't have to march.

On the far shore of the creek, the people marched for six more days. On the sixth day, they spotted an odd plant growing in the grass.

"This is corn," stated the leader. "Fetch logs and sticks, so we can make a fire and make a meal."

The people ate and felt quite happy.

The leader stuck his staff in a pile of stones that night. He stayed by the campfire and watched the sky. In the morning the staff was standing straight up.

"See how the staff stands straight! It knows that this is our home," he cried. "We will stay here and rest our tired feet. We will plant corn."

He held out a handful of corn seeds. The people felt glad to settle down. They were no longer displaced. They built new homes and planted corn seeds.

Soon, more corn was growing high and green. The people had a rich crop that could be made into many kinds of food. The leader had done his duty. "We will not starve any more," he smiled.

Comprehension Check

Summarize

Read "A Nation is Born" again. Then summarize the story.

Think About It

1. How did the leader find a place for the people to grow their own crops?

2. Why is a leader important to a large group of people?

3. How would you feel about following the leader after many hardships? Why?

4. Why might it be hard to find food and homes for a large group of people?

Write About It

Think about a problem in the world. If you were the President, how would you solve it?

Skills and Strategies

Decoding

Decode these words. What do you notice about the spellings?

morning	shirt	fern	thirsty
first	shore	weather	patterns
clever	clerk	acorns	never

Vocabulary

anxious	increased	observing
equipment	occur	method

Comprehension

SUMMARIZE When you summarize a story, you need to identify the main idea and details. Summarizing helps you understand a story.

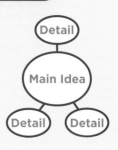

A Main Idea Web can help you find a main idea and supporting details to summarize a story.

Look for the main idea and details to help you summarize.

Weather Watchers

After lunch, Clover went to find her father. Thunder rumbled.

He was on the porch, observing the weather. Clover's dad had special equipment to take photos of storms. He waited for bad weather to occur. Then he went outside to take photos. This method made Clover anxious.

The thunder and rain increased. The wind swirled. Clover's dad took good photos.

Fill in the **Main Idea Web** for "Weather Watchers." Use the web to summarize the passage.

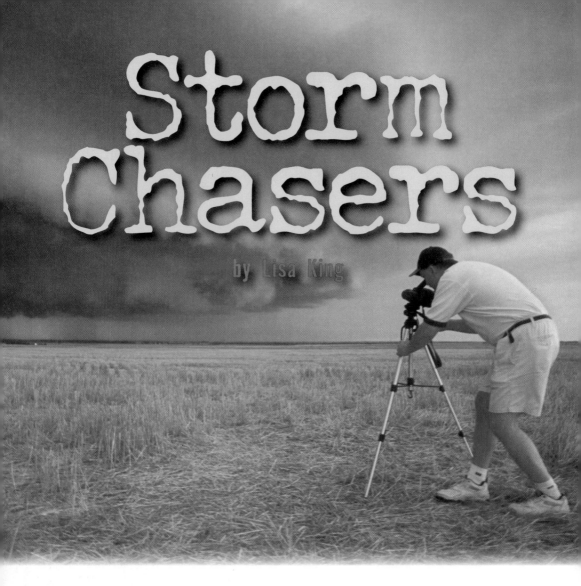

Storm Chasers

by Lisa King

Why do People Chase Storms?

"That's a neat job!" That is what most people say about storm chasing. Storm chasers try to get close to storms. They are anxious to watch and study them. But storm chasing is not an easy job. Storm chasers need to know a lot about the weather.

Storm chasing has increased during the last 40 years. Most storm chasers just like observing storms. Others take photos or make films of storms. Many chase storms because they love the adventure.

Tornado above a two-lane highway

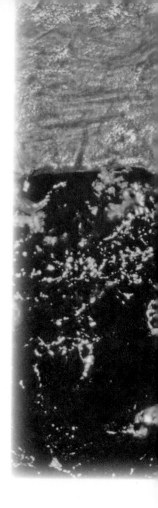

A storm chaser uses a laptop to track a storm.

Storm chasers need a lot of equipment. These tools include a cell phone and a camera with special film. Storm chasers use phones to make distress calls. Cameras are used to take photographs of storms.

Such photos are not easy to find, because most people will not get close to a storm. Storm chasers can sell good photos to magazines.

A radar map shows a hurricane approaching.

During the winter, storm chasers might read many books to find out more about storms. The best times to chase storms are during late spring and early fall.

Often, storms occur in the same spots. Storm chasers spend a lot of money to go all over the world. They may drive up to five hundred miles in a day to see a storm.

Storm chasers use every method to find storms. They follow weather news to find out where storm warnings have been declared.

A storm can cause serious flooding. Storms can harm people, crash cars, and knock houses over. Storms like these do not happen often.

Flood waters cover a bus and a house

Storm chasers and a film crew track an approaching storm.

What Do Storm Chasers Do?

Storm chasing is not always fun. Some days, storm chasers just sit in big fields all day. They watch the sky to find out if a storm will show up. Then they rush off to find the place the storm will hit.

Most storm chasing stops at night when storm chasers go home. Storm chasers don't want to be hit by a storm that they can't see.

Today, scientists know more about storms. But storm chasing is still a hard job. Chasers have to drive in heavy rain and high winds.

Some storms can cause lightning. People don't always know when lightning is about to strike. Sometimes they don't see it or hear it. Luckily, only a few chasers have been struck by lightning.

Lightning in a field

TV reporters track Hurricane Frances in Florida.

There are many ways to become a storm chaser. You might begin by reading about weather patterns. This may inspire you to become a reporter. Some people become known as TV weather reporters. They advise us about the weather daily.

Weather trackers in Australia

Storm chasing can be exciting, but it can also be hard work. You might be surprised at the information you can find by reading books about storms.

No matter which weather job you decide to do, make sure you read about it first. That way, you will be prepared. Storm chasing can be full of surprises!

Comprehension Check

Summarize

Read "Storm Chasers" again. Fill in your web, then use it to summarize the seletion.

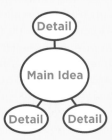

Think About It

1. Name three things that are important to a storm chaser. Explain your answer.

2. Why are a storm chaser's pictures so valuable?

3. Would you consider being a storm chaser? Why or why not?

4. How does being a storm chaser differ from being a weather reporter?

Write About It

Storm chasing is a hard job. Describe a safer way to take pictures of big storms.

Skills and Strategies

Decoding

Decode these words. What do you notice about the spellings?

nurse	first	return	purse
her	fur	hurt	girl
curb	turtle	purple	murmur

Vocabulary

required   disturb   enormous hurdles

Comprehension

DRAW CONCLUSIONS Authors don't always tell everything that happens. You have to use what you know and what the author does tell you to draw conclusions. Look for clues that support your conclusions.

Text Clues	Conclusion

A Conclusions Chart can help you find clues that support your conclusions.

Identify the text clues and conclusions.

A Gift for Uncle Burt

Uncle Burt gave Curtis an enormous set of blocks. When Curtis opened the box, he yelled, "You are the best uncle ever!"

Uncle Burt was getting older, and he got very sick. His doctor required him to stay in a nursing home. Curtis was running hurdles with his puppy when he heard. He wanted to visit Uncle Burt, and cheer him up.

Curtis asked a nurse, "May I bring in a puppy?" She smiled and said, "Yes, but don't disturb anyone!" He brought his puppy, Gordon. Uncle Burt grinned, "You are the best nephew ever!"

Use a **Conclusions Chart** to help you find clues and draw conclusions for "A Gift for Uncle Burt."

Uncle Bob and Nurse Turtle

by Eloise Jennings
illustrated by Stephanie Milanowski

Turtle's Big Visit

Uncle Bob had lived with Jim's family for years. But Uncle Bob required extra help now, so he moved to a nursing home. Before he moved, he gave Jim his books and his dog, Turtle. Turtle had thick golden fur. Jim always had a good time with Turtle.

"Jim, I need to cut your hair before we visit Uncle Bob," called Mom.

Jim did not like sitting still for a haircut. But he was anxious to talk to his mom about Uncle Bob.

"Do you think Uncle Bob misses us?" asked Jim.

"Yes, he does," said Mom. "But he has made friends at his new place, and we visit every week."

Jim got up and stretched his legs.
"When we went to see him last week,
everybody tried to talk to me. They
patted my head or pinched my cheek.
I felt bad. I wish I knew what to say to
them. I think they miss their old friends."

"Well, I have a surprise for you," Jim's mom said. "I spoke with Nurse Hill at the nursing home. She said that people can take their pets on visits, if they are careful. The pets just have to be neat and clean."

"Can we take Turtle?"

"Yes, Jim. Nurse Hill said that pets can make people feel better."

"Turtle, come here girl! We're going to visit Uncle Bob!" Jim got Turtle's leash and led her to the curb.

When Jim, Mom, and Dad got to the nursing home, Turtle sprang out of the car. She ran straight for the door. It seemed that she knew she was going to see Uncle Bob.

A Promise to Return

Jim didn't see Uncle Bob when he first walked in. Turtle did. She gave a quick bark. Then she ran over to the window where Uncle Bob sat. He leaned down to pet her, and Turtle's tail wagged fast.

"How did you get Turtle in here? I hope she won't disturb people!" said Uncle Bob. But he had an enormous smile.

"Nurse Hill told us that we could bring her to visit," declared Jim. The excitement in the room increased when Turtle showed up. Mom had packed a ball in her purse for Turtle to play with.

Nurse Hill stopped by. Jim asked her why it was possible for pets to visit nursing homes.

"That's simple," she told Jim. "Having a pet around makes people happy. When people are happier, their bodies get stronger."

Jim rubbed Turtle's head. He said, "I'm going to have to start calling you Nurse Turtle!"

Jim promised to visit again soon. Uncle Bob made him promise to bring Turtle.

"I will," said Jim. "Next time, let's go outside. Then, we can set up hurdles for Turtle to jump over. We'll see you on Saturday."

Uncle Bob said with a joyful grin, "I'll bring my camera. We'll take photos. I'll see you and Turtle on Saturday."

Comprehension Check

Summarize

Read "Uncle Bob and Nurse Turtle" again. Then summarize the story.

Think About It

1. Could you tell that Uncle Bob was lonely? Use details from the story to fill in your chart.

2. How do pets (or wild animals) make people feel?

3. Think about a time when you felt lonely. What cheered you up?

Text Clues	Conclusion

4. Animals can help people in many ways. Pick one way and describe it.

Write About It

If you could have any animal as a pet, which one would you pick and why? Write a paragraph about this pet.

Skills and Strategies

Decoding

Decode these words. What do you notice about the spellings?

blur	shook	woods	footnote
goodbye	stood	burn	book
look	cookie	took	surf

Vocabulary

faint	unfamiliar	website
wisdom	approaches	

Comprehension

DRAW CONCLUSIONS Authors don't always tell everything that happens. You have to use what you know and what the author does tell you to draw conclusions. Look for clues that support your conclusions.

Text Clues	Conclusion

A Conclusions Chart can help you find clues that support your conclusions.

Identify the text clues and conclusions.

Mrs. Cook and her Class

Mrs. Cook asked her class to try an unfamiliar task. She passed out papers that showed hand signals. She explained that this was the sign language alphabet.

Mrs. Cook said that most deaf people use hand signals to communicate. Some deaf people can hear faint sounds, but many cannot hear at all.

The class looked at a website on approaches to teaching. It talked about the wisdom behind sign language.

Use a **Conclusions Chart** to help you find clues and draw conclusions for "Mrs. Cook and her Class."

A Closer Look

by Louis Stater
illustrated by Amy Tucker

Brooke Meets Liz

"I miss my old friends. What if there are no kids my age here?"

Brooke's family knew that she would make more friends. But Brooke was still upset. She sat on a rock in her garden by the woods. There were no kids in sight. Then, she spotted an older girl. "Hi," yelled Brooke. "My family just moved in."

The girl made a faint sound. Then, she made an unfamiliar motion with her hands. What was wrong? "She's deaf," thought Brooke. Brooke didn't want to seem rude, but she didn't know how to speak with the girl. So she waved goodbye and hurried back inside her home. The girl just stood still. She seemed hurt.

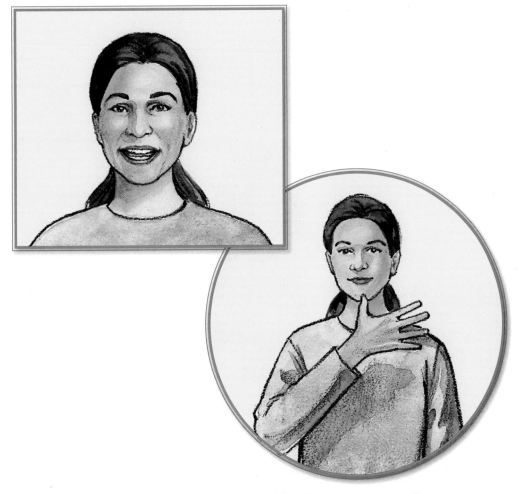

This sign means *mother.*

"Mom," said Brooke at lunch. "I think the girl next door is deaf."

"Yes," replied Brooke's mom. "Her name is Liz. I invited her to visit us later."

"How will I speak to her?" asked Brooke.

After lunch, Mom knocked on Brooke's door. Brooke was curled up reading a book. "I don't mean to disturb you. Do you have time to look at a website with me?" asked her mom. "I think it may help you understand Liz." Brooke put down her book.

The first article on the website discussed two men who lived back in the 1800s. Their names were Alexander Graham Bell and Edward Gallaudet. Their lives were very much alike. Their fathers were teachers of the deaf. Their mothers were deaf. Each man married a deaf woman.

Alexander Graham Bell

Edward Gallaudet

Lip-Reading and Sign Language

These men knew they had the wisdom to help deaf people. But Bell and Gallaudet took different approaches to teaching them.

Bell felt that it would be most helpful to teach a deaf person to read lips. Gallaudet felt that it would be better to teach deaf people to use sign language. Both men looked for the best method of teaching the deaf.

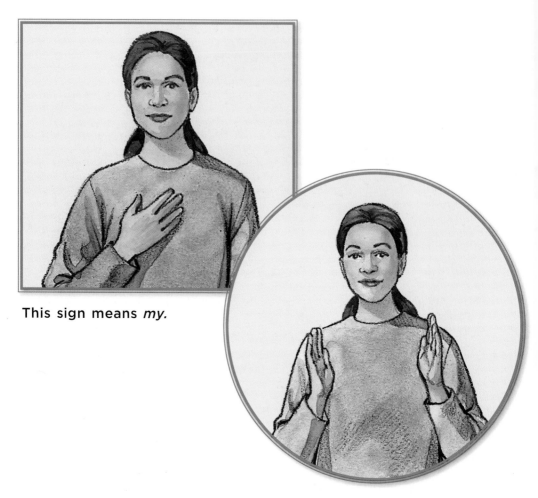

This sign means *my.*

The sign means *house.*

The website's footnotes stated that it doesn't take long to learn a few signs. This made Brooke feel good. But she knew it would not be simple.

Practice is required to become good at sign language. Each letter of a word can be spelled out with the fingers. Some people can spell sixty words in a minute.

Brooke really liked the next article. Deaf children wrote about sign language. Over 1,000,000 deaf and hearing people use it. Many people say that it is more fun to learn than foreign languages. People who sign also use eye, face, head, and body movements to communicate.

There were pictures of children signing with each other on the website. Brooke and her mom were glad that they had looked at the website.

The sign means *very.*

The sign means *big.*

When Liz came over, she seemed happy. Brooke was shy about using her new skill. She signed, "hello." Liz smiled and signed "hello" back. That's when their friendship started!

Liz helped Brooke practice sign language. They became best friends!

Comprehension Check

Summarize

Read "A Closer Look" again. Then summarize the story.

Think About It

1. How did Brooke's feelings about Liz change throughout the story? Use details from the story to fill in your chart.

Text Clues	Conclusion

2. Why is it important for people to learn about different physical challenges?

3. Describe how you might feel in a country where you didn't know the language.

4. Explain why it might be hard for Liz to make friends in a new place.

Write About It

Imagine that you lost the ability to speak. List ways you could communicate with your family and friends.

Skills and Strategies

Decoding

Decode these words. What do you notice about the spellings?

pools	shook	groom	goodbye
tools	oozed	bloom	choose
toothbrush	footnote	spoons	goop

Vocabulary

decayed	experts	composed
solution	environment	

Comprehension

PERSUASION Persuasion is used by authors to get other people to agree with their ideas or opinions. Identifying persuasion can help you understand a story.

Word or Phrase	Technique

Use a Persuasion Chart to help you figure out how the author uses persuasion.

Identify the clues about persuasion.

The Problem with Oil

We must all make choices about energy. Some people use carpooling. This helps save oil. Oil is a kind of fuel. It is composed of decayed animals and plants.

The reason we try to save oil is simple. There are only a few oil sources. Oil is not renewable. If it is used up, we will not have it to use for lights or cars.

Experts say that oil harms the environment. It makes the air dirty. This hurts plants and animals. There is a solution to this problem. We must use less oil.

Fill in the **Persuasion Chart** for "The Problem with Oil." Then use it to help you summarize the passage.

Oil: From Fuels to Tools

by Eliza Wang

Fossil Fuels

Fossil fuels started a long time ago. Plants and animals died and fell deep into the sea. There, they decayed in the dark water. Layers of sand and clay covered them. These layers became rocks. The rocks pressed hard on the plants and animals. The decayed plants and animals turned into coal, oil, or natural gas. This took millions of years. Gas is composed of these plants and animals.

In the 1800's, oil lamps and candles were used for lighting around the world.

People started using oil over six thousand years ago. Fishermen and traders rubbed oil on parts of their boats. This kept the boats from sinking in the water.

Later, oil helped armies. They marched in cold, wet snow. The soldiers used oil to protect their boots from harsh weather. During the 1800s, oil was known as the best fuel for lamps.

In the Middle East, oil oozed up from the desert in pools. They used it for heat and light. In North America, Native Americans lifted oil from water with blankets. They used it as medicine. The American settlers used it as fuel in their lamps.

In 1859 in Pennsylvania, Edwin L. Drake found a way to drill through rocks and strike oil. He used a well to pump up the oil. Drake's method of pumping oil is still used today.

Edwin L. Drake (on the right) on the site of the world's first successful oil well

Oil rigs like this one are used to drill oil in the ocean.

Oil lies far below the top layer of dirt. Drills
are used to reach the oil. It is pumped up by rigs.
Charts of rock layers help people choose where
to put the rigs. Some rigs are set up in the sea.
From rigs, oil travels through pipes. Then it is
shipped to big factories.

Oil and Toothbrushes

Oil has many uses. Did you know that plastic is made from oil? Most toothbrushes, milk cartons, and plastic spoons started as oil. Factories change the thick, black goop into a lot of things. One of those things is the liquid gas used to run cars, ships, and planes.

Cars use a lot of gas. Scientists are looking for cleaner fuels, such as fuel made from corn.

Polar bears, foxes, wolves, and reindeer all live in the Arctic.

Our country gets a big part of its oil from other countries. We do not have enough oil at home to fill our enormous needs. Oil has been found in the Arctic. Some people think we should drill there. Others do not think this is a good idea. They think it might harm the environment and the wildlife.

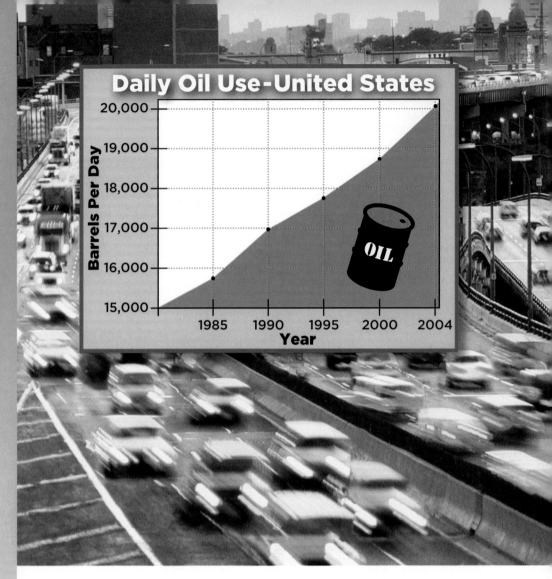

Daily Oil Use–United States

Rush hour happens in the morning and evening each weekday.

Experts think that we have only enough oil on Earth to last sixty more years. That time is approaching soon. When that oil is used up, there will be no more for millions of years. That is one reason we need to cut back our use of oil. We also need to look for more energy sources.

Walking to school saves gas, and it is a great way to exercise.

We can all do our part. There are simple ways to use less oil. We will need less if we don't drive as much. Walking or riding a bike to school can help. We can set our heaters to far lower settings. We can turn off lights when we don't require them. Another useful idea is recycling plastic items made from oil.

People have used windmills to create power for more than two thousand years.

Fossil fuels make up around 95% of the world's energy resources. But the reserve is shrinking. We could help if we all start using less oil. Some think we can use more energy from the sun, wind, and water. These forms of energy are renewable. If we all help, we can find a solution together!

Comprehension Check

Summarize

Read "Oil: From Fuels to Tools" again. Then summarize the selection.

Think About It

1. What does the author want you to think about using oil? Use details from the selection to fill in your chart.

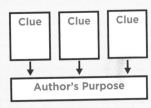

2. Why is it important for humans to conserve oil?

3. Describe how you can help conserve energy at home.

4. Should we drill for oil in the Arctic? List some reasons for and against.

Write About It

List some of the ways you use oil or oil products each day. How might your life be different without them?

Skills and Strategies

Decoding

Decode these words. What do you notice about the spellings?

coil	tomboy	cartoon	enjoy
avoid	toy	spool	poison
noise	loose	oil	destroy

Vocabulary

motion	coil	liquid
massive	avoid	

Comprehension

SEQUENCE Sequence is the order in which events in a story take place. Understanding sequence helps you understand the story.

Figure out the most important events in sequence. Use your Sequence Chart to help you.

Identify the sequence of events.

Whales and Dolphins

Last week, my family went to the sea. The sea is a massive body of water where many animals live. The motion of these animals makes the sea come alive!

This week, we went to the zoo. We saw dolphins and whales. They like playing with humans. They made clicking noises and sprayed coils of water at us!

Then a zookeeper talked about the sea. He said that when we dump poisonous liquids in the sea, we make animals sick. We must avoid doing anything that might harm these animals.

Fill in the **Sequence Chart** for "Whales and Dolphins." Then use it to retell the passage.

Humpback Whales

by Sam Matthews
illustrated by Nancy King

Voices from the Sea

Whales spend their lives in the sea. But it might be helpful to know that whales are not fish. Whales have lungs. Whales have hair and are warm-blooded. Their young weigh three thousand pounds when they are born. They drink one hundred pounds of milk each day. Maybe that's why these babies gain as much as two hundred pounds a day!

Humpback whales live in every sea. They can weigh as much as ninety thousand pounds. That's as heavy as thirty cars.

These whales can live fifty years. Scientists can tell a whale's age by looking in its ears. Rings form in the wax that builds up inside their ears. Scientists check the number of rings to find out a whale's age.

When this whale jumps out of the water, it arches or humps its back. This is why it's called *humpback.* The whale has a big flipper on each side of its body. Flippers help steer the whale.

They're also known for big bumps on their mouths, with a hair growing from each one. These hairs help the whale sense motion and find fish.

Whales breathe through two blowholes on their backs. Whales can close the holes when they dive deep into the water. Scientists say that whales can hold their breath underwater up to twenty minutes. When they resurface to breathe, whales shoot air and water from the blowholes. This spray can shoot as high as ten feet into the air.

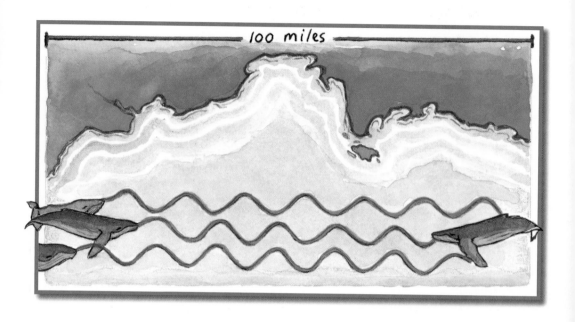

Enjoying Humpback Whales

Male humpback whales sing songs! Their songs start with a faint hum. The noises become louder, and might last up to 20 minutes. You can hear whale songs 20 miles away. If you dove underwater, you could hear the noise from 100 miles away.

Experts don't know why the whales sing. Some think they are trying to make contact. But many people say the whale songs bring them joy.

Whales sometimes hunt food in groups. Humpback whales join up underwater. When they come upon a school of fish, one whale swims in a circle. Then, it blows a coil of bubbles. The bubbles confuse the fish and cause them to swim to the surface. Then, the whales swim up and quickly eat a big meal.

Humpback whales do not have teeth. But there is a solution. They have strong hairs that hang from their upper jaws. These hairs are called baleen. The baleen is made of the same material as our hair and nails. They strain food through these strong hairs. The baleen lets liquid drain out and stores fish inside the whale's mouth.

Being massive does not keep these whales safe. The sea has become less safe for humpback whales in the past thirty years. Boats spill oil and poisons in the sea, which can make the whales sick. People also throw trash in the sea. It is hard for the whales to avoid oil and trash. Humpback whales need help from both scientists and people.

Scientists enjoy studying these creatures and their songs. They've got good reasons for keeping whales safe. Today, the humpback whale and its environment are protected by law.

Many people say they'll never get tired of watching these whales. Humpback whales are gentle. The whales swim right up to boats and divers. People like humpback whales, and humpback whales like people!

Comprehension Check

Summarize

Read "Humpback Whales" again. Then summarize the selection.

Think About It

1. Retell, in your own words, how whales hunt when they hunt as a group. Use details from the selection to fill in your chart.

2. Why is it important for humans to avoid throwing trash in the sea?

3. What sea animal trait would be most helpful to you? Why?

4. How is the way humans breathe different from the way whales breathe?

Write About It

What can humans do to make sure we do not harm animals? Explain your ideas.

Skills and Strategies

Decoding

Decode these words. What do you notice about the spellings?

already	cause	joy	crawl
pause	walnut	shawl	fault
spoil	small	claw	tomboy

Vocabulary

retreats	supply
brittle	established

Comprehension

COMPARE AND CONTRAST

Comparing is telling how things or people are alike. Contrasting is telling how they are different. Comparing and contrasting will help you understand the story.

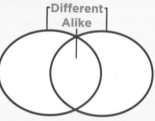

Use the Venn Diagram to compare and contrast.

Compare and contrast crabs and castles.

Crabs and Castles

Did you ever make a sandcastle at the beach? You may have hunted for pretty shells to put on the walls. It did not seem brittle until you saw how the tide retreated and increased. One big wave washed it away!

Small crabs also make things in the sand. These crabs dig homes as carefully as we make cars. A crab spends days shaping the sand with its claws. It tries to build near a food supply. The home is finished, until a wave washes up and destroys it! The crab's established space is lost.

Fill in the **Venn Diagram** for "Crabs and Castles." Use the diagram to retell the passage.

The Rise and Fall of Tides

by Miles Jones

WHAT CAUSES TIDES?

Did you ever visit the seashore? Did you go at high tide? That's when seawater covers most of the beach. Then, a change happens at low tide. The seawater retreats into the sea. You can walk on the beach once more. Most beaches have two high tides and two low tides every 24 hours.

Tides are caused by the pull of gravity between Earth, the Moon, and the Sun. The Moon is closer to our world, Earth. So, the Moon's pull is stronger. The Moon's pull causes the seas to push outward. These strong outward pushes cause high tides. When there are no outward pushes, it is low tide.

When the moon is full or new, high tides are higher and low tides are lower.

A trawler is a kind of fishing boat. This trawler is followed by hungry seagulls.

People who fish keep a watch on the tides. The movement of the water carries their boats and trawlers in and out. When the tide goes out, the fishermen leave port to fish. When the tide comes in, they return home again.

People like to find shells on the shore. They dive deep into the sea to see a coral reef. They need to know about tides. The best time for finding shells is low tide, because the water isn't as high. Reef divers must make pre-dive checks on tides. Tides can make the sea too deep or unsafe to dive.

High tide and big storms, like hurricanes, wash piles of sea shells onto the beach.

The size of the tides depends upon how the shore is shaped. In some places, the tide can spread out. Then it may only rise a few inches each day. In other places, there is no room for the tide to spread out. Then it might rise an extra ten or twenty feet.

HIGH TIDE
The sea at high tide can be over 50 feet higher than at low tide.

LOW TIDE
The biggest tidal range is at Bay of Fundy, Canada.

The first power station to use energy from the tides is on the Rance River in France.

TIDES AND ENERGY

Tides can be used to supply energy. Some places have already established power plants by the sea. They use tides to manufacture electricity. A wall of water runs through a dam during high tide. It spins engines to make electricity. Water runs back out through the dam during low tide. It turns the engines again.

Sea stars live both in the sea and in tide pools. If a sea star loses an arm, it can grow another!

Tides can be helpful. They bring plenty of food and air to the animals. Small plants and animals make homes in tide pools. Tide pools are holes in the sea's sandy bottom. Tide pools are formed and refilled by the motion of tides. You might find a sea star or a crab with big claws in a tide pool.

The tides can cause strong waves. These massive waves crash over the animals. This may keep a small sea creature underwater. It may push animals out of the water. In the end, the animals wash up on land. They become dry and brittle. Animals might crawl deep into the moist sand for safety.

Ghost crabs dig tunnels up to three feet deep. They live on the East Coast of the United States.

People explore the tide pools along a beach at Olympic National Park, Washington.

How can we help animals living near our shores? We can be careful when we pick up the animals we find there. We can leave shells and rocks at the shore. Rocks often provide safety from other animals and the tides. We can be careful not to destroy animals' homes. We only visit the seashore. But the animals live there. We should help them enjoy a safe and clean environment.

Comprehension Check

Summarize

Read "The Rise and Fall of Tides" again. Then summarize the selection.

Think About It

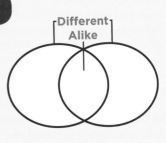

Different
Alike

1. What is the same and different about low and high tides? Use details to fill in your chart.

2. Why is it important to understand tides?

3. What can you do to help keep beaches, parks, or other public areas clean?

4. Reread p. 148 of "César Chávez: Righting a Wrong." How does Chávez's work compare with the work of people who keep the environment clean?

Write About It

Do you think it is important to keep our seas and seashores safe and clean? Explain.

Skills and Strategies

Decoding

Decode these words. What do you notice about the spellings?

stretch	string	splash	stripe
scratch	sprout	scream	splinter
include	split	scrape	explain

Vocabulary

assistance	project	sketch
perform	positive	

Comprehension

SUMMARIZE When you summarize, include only the important parts of a story. Details do not belong in a summary.

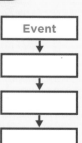

A Summarizing Chart can help you identify important events and keep track of them.

Look for the main idea and details to help you summarize.

A Helpful Project

Springfield Animal Shelter gave assistance to hundreds of animals. Then a peculiar thing happened. The shelter would have to close.

Mr. Strand's class set up a project to help the shelter. Brett promised to sketch posters. Ashton and Chrissy chose to perform a short play.

The class was positive they could help, and they were right. People loved the play and sketches, and gave money to the shelter. It stayed open so people could keep helping animals.

Fill in the **Summarizing Chart** for "A Helpful Project." Use the chart to summarize the passage.

Stephanie's Lesson

by Pearl Roy
illustrated by Cynthia McGrellis

Ashton and Tracy

I like to work and study by myself. I was shocked when my teacher asked me to plan a project with two boys instead. I tried to change her mind. But Miss Boyd was positive that I would enjoy working with them. I doubted that! Ashton and Tracy just goof off and talk about sports. They don't get things finished.

Miss Boyd sent Ashton, Tracy, and me to the library. We had to do a project on helping others.

We looked for ideas in books and articles. We even asked Mr. Strand, the library teacher, for assistance. He is helpful. But choosing a project that all of us liked was not going to be easy!

We retreated to a table to talk about ideas. Tracy and Ashton started being silly. I tried to get them to talk to me. They just kept whispering to each other. They tried to avoid me. Each time I started talking, the boys put their hands over their ears. They looked at me in their peculiar way. I finally gave up.

"Fine!" I yelled. "I'll do the project by myself!"

"No, Stephanie," said Tracy. "Just listen. Ashton's a good actor. I'm good at art. You're a good writer. Let's do something fun."

"Let's put on a play for our class," said Ashton. Then he grabbed a hat from a shelf. He put it on and started to perform. It really was funny.

Mr. Strand came to see him. "I'm thinking about starting a story hour," he said. "I'm positive that the first grade kids would like it. Ashton, would you like to perform?"

"Wait!" I cried. "Mr. Strand, will you let us plan the story hour for next week?"

"That's a great idea," said Ashton and Tracy.

A Perfect Project

Mr. Strand thought before he gave an answer. "Well, I planned on telling the stories myself. But you are funny, Ashton. I will include you three in the storytelling on Monday afternoon."

We ran to tell Miss Boyd. "We're going to tell a story to the first graders next week." Miss Boyd told us it was a good project for us.

After school, we stood on my porch. We joked and laughed for a while. Then we went in and got to work.

We chose to retell a fairy tale with stuffed animals. My job was rewriting the story. Tracy's job was painting the background. Ashton's job was telling the story and acting out the parts. We had a good plan.

The next day, we returned to the library
with supplies to preset our stage. We took toys
and old dress-up clothes from home. Mr. Strand
helped Tracy put paper on a back wall. Tracy had
plenty of room to sketch pictures.

Then we practiced until we could easily tell
the stories. Ashton even added splashing and
squawking noises, for fun.

Monday afternoon finally came. We were a hit! The first graders liked us. We had a good time, too.

Ashton, Tracy, and I learned about helping others. We also learned how to tell a story. But the most important thing we learned was how to work together. I might even be willing to work with those boys again!

Comprehension Check

Summarize

Read "Stephanie's Lesson" again. Then fill in the Summarizing Chart. When you finish, use the chart to help you summarize the story.

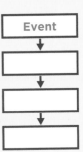

Think About It

1. What made Stephanie realize that working in a group can be helpful?

2. Why is it important to listen to others?

3. What do you like about working with others? Why?

4. Think of a difficult task you accomplished by yourself. What would have been different if you worked with someone else?

Write About It

Think of a time you worked with someone with different views. Were you able to work together well? If not, what could you have done differently?

Skills and Strategies

Decoding

Decode these words. What do you notice about the spellings?

town	screen	count	brown
about	spread	shout	now
split	loudly	around	down

Vocabulary

lawn	lovely	funds
split	fabulous	ingredients

Comprehension

MAKE JUDGMENTS You learn about characters by thinking about what they say and do. This can help you make judgments about characters.

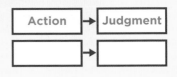

A Make Judgments Chart can help you understand the characters in a story.

Read

What judgments can you make about the characters?

Howie Fixes the Lawn

The lawn in front of Howie's school did not look lovely. The hot sun had dried the grass to a pale shade of yellow.

Howie asked Scout, "How can we fix the school's lawn?" Scout said, "We need to think of a way to raise funds. We can fix it up then."

Howie said, "Maybe we can have a bake sale!" They went to see the principal, Mr. Dowd. He thought it was a fine plan. He would help them get ingredients.

Howie and Scout split the work with people who wanted to help. Mr. Dowd told the boys, "Now the lawn will look fabulous!"

Fill in the **Make Judgments Chart** for "Howie Fixes the Lawn." Use the chart to summarize the passage.

Miss Brown's Class Helps Out

by Don Ungar
illustrated by Ralph Canaday

Job Day in Miss Brown's Class

Place: MISS BROWN'S classroom.

MISS BROWN: Let's thank Bob's dad for coming to Job Day. Now we understand what it's like to make and sell ice cream.

(Students clap loudly.)

HOWIE: The best part is that you get to taste all the ice cream!

BOB'S DAD: We do more tasting than that. We sample the ingredients we need from local farms before we buy them. We scout out the best stuff.

KIM: That sounds like fun!

BOB'S DAD: I have a treat for all of you. Each of these cards is good for a free ice-cream cone.

ALL: Wow! Thanks!

(Bob's Dad leaves.)

JILL: Wouldn't it be faster for them to get stuff in town? It must take hours to drive to those farms!

BOB: Dad says they can count on farmers for the freshest ingredients. Then the ice cream tastes better.

KIM: Job Day was fun. I liked last week's, too. Kay's mom told us about her job as a nurse.

HOWIE: She works at a hospital helping sick kids. It sounds like they have a hard time.

WALT: Can we do something to make them feel better? Maybe we can give them toys. I have a drum and trumpet I can bring.

JILL: They make too much noise! Maybe we should all bring in some of our books.

DAN: We can bring DVDs. I bet they would like to see some movies!

HOWIE: Why don't we have a party for them? We can each bring a game or book.

DAN: Don't forget movies!

MIKE: And we can turn in our ice-cream cards and bring them ice cream!

MISS BROWN: That sounds like a great project. How many kids are there? We have twenty cards.

KAY (frowning): Mom said there were fifty kids in her hospital.

BOB: We'd need thirty more cards. We can buy more from my dad.

KAY: But how? We need money.

WALT (shouts): I know! Let's draw ice-cream cards and take them to shops in town. The shopkeepers might be helpful and sell the cards for us. We'll explain that buying a card will buy ice cream for those kids. Then, we'll buy real cards from Bob's dad!

MISS BROWN: Great! Let's draw!

Time: One hour later.

MISS BROWN *(looking around)*: Nice work, class.

HOWIE: Looking at these sketches is making my stomach growl! Will we make enough money to buy supplies for the party?

MISS BROWN: I think so. Let's meet on the school lawn tomorrow. We'll split up and take our drawings out to the shops.

KIM: My mouth is watering. I hope there's some ice cream at my house.

WALT: Just wait until the party!

The Class Goes To Town

Place: Downtown Bike Shop. Time: Next day.

KAY: Our class is raising funds to help sick kids. Can you sell our ice-cream cones?

MR. DOWD: I don't have a freezer!

KAY: You don't need a freezer. We've drawn them.

DAN: They are low in fat, and they are not overpriced!

MR. DOWD: That's fabulous! You can leave ten with me.

Place: South Street Bookshop.

DAWN: Can you sell our ice cream here?

MISS CROWN: No ice cream in this shop, please.

LUKE: How about this kind of ice cream? (*Shows cards.*) They're cards to get treats for sick kids.

MISS CROWN: How lovely! I've never seen a blue banana split before. I can sell five. (*She puts them on the counter.*)

Place: MISS BROWN'S classroom. Time: Three days later.

DAN: Mr. Dowd said everyone who saw our drawings wanted to buy one!

MISS BROWN: Have you counted up the money, Dan?

DAN: Yes! We have enough for thirty cards. So with our twenty cards, all fifty kids will get ice cream.

WALT: And we each brought books and toys from home. We have lots of things for kids to play with.

DAN: And movies to look at!

MISS BROWN: I'm proud of you, class.

(Bob's Dad comes in with a bag.)

BOB'S DAD: Hi kids. I have your cards. And look what else I have. *(He takes out a big tub of strawberries.)*

JILL: Are these berries from a farm?

BOB'S DAD: Yes! The farmer wanted you to have them to go with the ice cream.

JILL: *(tastes a berry)* These are really good. Now I get it! Farmers help you make better ice cream.

BOB: Thanks, Dad! You should come to our party, too!

MISS BROWN: I think the kids will be happy.

HOWIE: We'll have books, games, DVDs, and ice cream. It will be a really good party!

JILL: Don't forget the strawberries!

Comprehension Check

Summarize

Read "Miss Brown's Class Helps Out" again.
Then summarize the story in your own words.

Think About It

1. Do you think that the class's decision to sell ice cream cards was a good idea? Use details from the story to fill in your chart.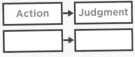

2. Why is it important for people to help each other?

3. Think about something helpful that you could do for someone today. Describe what you would do.

4. How else could the class have helped the children at the hospital?

Write About It

Describe a time you felt good after helping someone. What did you do? How did the other person respond?

Skills and Strategies

Decoding

Decode these words. What do you notice about the spellings?

center	acid	germ	pencil
city	gentle	distance	danger
gym	cellar	orange	region

Vocabulary

taming   advanced   estimated

achievement   courage

Comprehension

FACT AND OPINION A fact is something that can be proven to be true. An opinion is based on someone's feelings. Understanding fact and opinion helps you understand the story.

Fact	Opinion

A Fact and Opinion Chart can help you find the facts and opinions in a story.

270

Look for the facts and opinions.

Taming the Wild

Humans have spent many years exploring new places. Long ago, exploring was difficult. Science was very simple, and most tools were not advanced.

Most explorers estimated times and distances. Ships sailed off to find new worlds without a plan or a map. These explorers faced great danger. It took courage to be an explorer.

Even today, people are still taming wild places. We send explorers deep into the sea and up into space. These explorers are still very brave, and their exploring is a great achievement.

Fill in the **Fact and Opinion Chart** for "Taming the Wild." Then use the chart to retell the passage.

The Edge of the World!

by Jeremy Bluett

Racing for the North Pole

Robert Peary was an explorer with a dream. He wanted to stand on the North Pole. Many people said Peary's dream was foolish. The North Pole was too cold for humans, and the winters were too dark. How would he get there? Many thought ships could not cut through the thick winter ice.

Robert Peary with his dogs aboard his ship, *The Roosevelt,* during his race to the Pole

When Peary decided to reach the North Pole, he spent years making his plan. He had to study how to sail the sea. He had to learn how to store food for a long time. He also learned to use sled dogs.

He knew this would be a long and hard trip. He estimated that it would take years. He also needed another explorer to help him. Peary called on Matthew Henson for assistance.

273

Robert Peary's ship, *The Roosevelt*, two miles below Cape Sheridan in the Arctic, 1908

Peary and Henson designed and built a special ship with their funds. They knew they would have to sail during the summer. Then the ice would be easier to split. They could plow through the Arctic ice and make the trip faster. They would be able to bear the coldest weather. Then they could spend the winter in the Arctic water.

Peary and Henson understood that going to the North Pole was too hard for just two men. They took with them a large number of helpers. These helpers came from local villages in Greenland. They brought their best sled dogs with them.

During the winter, they would make sleds. They would make fur clothing and mittens, and train the sled dogs.

Peary's team used sled dogs to reach the North Pole. Depending on the distance of the trip, two to fifteen dogs might pull one sled.

Danger on the Ice

Peary had planned his trip to the North Pole carefully. His team sailed for days, taming the waves, the ice, and the tides. They finally arrived at a stopping place to set up a base camp.

From the base camp, Peary, Henson, and the helpers traveled in stages. They stopped to rest along the way. This kept the men and sled dogs in top shape.

Peary used base camps like this one to rest along the way.

When they reached the last stopping place, Peary and Henson decided to go on with a smaller team. They only took four helpers with them, and set out to the North Pole. They took light sleds and the best dogs. Luckily, the weather was good, and they could travel fast. Soon, they reached the North Pole.

Arctic ice near the North Pole

An igloo on sea ice near the Arctic

As soon as they arrived, the explorers raced back to the ship. They ran like racehorses rushing to the finish line. Although the weather was still nice, they feared being caught in a storm. They were 400 miles out in the water and in danger of losing their lives. Luckily, the weather stayed clear. Peary, Henson, and their helpers arrived safely back at the base camp.

A few weeks later, Peary and Henson came home and became famous explorers. At the time, some doubted their achievement. It seemed like an impossible task. But today's advanced tools prove that these brave men did reach the North Pole.

Peary and his team were welcomed home by crowds of people.

Peary and his team at the North Pole, April 1909

Peary and Henson traveled through ice and wind to get to the North Pole. They were the first to place an American flag there. It took a lot of planning and courage. Some people still think of Peary and Henson as the bravest American explorers of all time.

Robert Peary Timeline

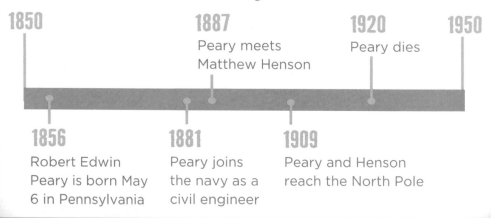

1850

1887
Peary meets
Matthew Henson

1920
Peary dies

1950

1856
Robert Edwin
Peary is born May
6 in Pennsylvania

1881
Peary joins
the navy as a
civil engineer

1909
Peary and Henson
reach the North Pole

Comprehension Check

Summarize

Read "The Edge of the World!" again. Then summarize the selection.

Think About It

1. Find facts and opinions in the selection. Put each in the correct column on your chart.

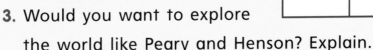

Fact	Opinion

2. How do explorers contribute to the world?

3. Would you want to explore the world like Peary and Henson? Explain.

4. How might the planning and experiences of an explorer in the rain forest differ from Peary's planning and experiences?

Write About It

Pretend you are an explorer. What part of the world would you explore? Describe the plans you would need to make.

Skills and Strategies

Decoding

Decode these words. What do you notice about the spellings?

model	fable	jungle	tunnel
trouble	panel	middle	towel
squirrel	puzzle	travel	able

Vocabulary

skills	admire	discovered
capable	flexible	mumbled

Comprehension

CHARACTER A character's feelings can change. Character traits are longer lasting. Thinking about a character's traits will help you understand why a character acts a certain way.

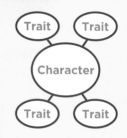

A Character Web can help you figure out character traits.

What traits does Rachel have? Use the way she acts to help you figure out her traits.

Rachel Cook, Artist

When Rachel was little, her mom took her to see art. Rachel began to admire the skills of the artists. Rachel started drawing her pet goldfish and birds.

When Rachel got older, she went to art camp. On the first day, she discovered that it was far away from home. When the teacher asked her a question, Rachel mumbled. Rachel missed her pets. What else could she draw?

The teacher hugged Rachel, and said she was a capable artist. She took Rachel on walks and helped her draw squirrels and deer. Rachel learned to be flexible. She was happy to be an artist!

Use a **Character Web** to help you figure out Rachel's character traits.

A Challenge for Chen

by Danielle Upton

illustrated by Yangsook Choi

Chen's Travels

One night, Chen was eating dinner with his mom and dad.

"I have big news," Chen's dad said. "In three weeks, we will move to a new town."

Chen's face fell. "How far away will we move?" he asked.

"We are only moving fifty miles away. We will be much closer to my new job," Chen's dad said.

"We'll be near your job, but fifty miles is far from the zoo," Chen mumbled.

Chen liked playing baseball. He liked doing puzzles, too. But he liked drawing animals best of all. He liked the feel of the paper beneath his pencil. He liked seeing birds and bobcats take shape in the middle of his notebook pages.

Chen had started drawing animals when he was seven. Now he was ten. His drawing skills got more and more advanced, and Chen knew why. It was because of the time he spent at the zoo.

The city zoo was near Chen's house. Each weekend he took his notebook and pencil and went there to draw.

First he loosened up his hand by drawing circles. Then he sat by the cages and watched the animals. He saw how they moved and how they ate. As he watched, he sketched them in his book. The more he watched, the more capable he became.

The best part of the zoo was Tiger Town. Its tall green grass made it look like a jungle. Chen waited for the tigers to curl up and fall asleep. Then he carefully drew them.

When he came home, Chen copied his pictures on clean paper. He painted them and taped them up in his room. Purples, pinks, browns, and greens filled his walls. Chen liked looking at each picture before he went to sleep at night.

The zoo was Chen's favorite place in the world. But now there would be no more weekly zoo trips. How could Chen's family travel that far each week?

Chen sadly took down all his pictures from his walls. Then he packed his drawing book in a trunk. "I will not be able to draw animals now," he said to himself. He hid his book under a pile of towels.

Chen's New Models

Chen put his zoo pictures up on his wall in his new room. He missed the zoo and his animal friends.

Then, Chen's mom and dad found his notebook.

"I am sad you stopped drawing, Chen," said Dad. "It was a big achievement."

"I didn't want to stop," Chen said. "But how can I draw here? There are no animals."

Just then, Mitten the cat tickled Chen's leg. Chen held out a rice ball for Mitten to nibble.

Dad chuckled. "No animals here, you say?"

"You need to be more flexible, Chen," Mom said, grinning. "Make the most of what you have."

A big smile spread across Chen's face. "Mom, where is the drawing paper?"

"I have a sheet right here," she said.

Chen put his paper on the floor by Mitten. It felt good to have a pencil back in his hand.

"Mitten is so still," said Mom. "I think she knows she is your model."

Chen's pencil danced on the page. Soon
he had finished his drawing. Then he painted
in Mitten's creamy fur. Mom and Dad smiled.

When Chen had finished painting, he jumped
up. "If I found one animal, maybe I can find
others!" he said.

Chen went outside. He found a squirrel in a
tree. A turtle swam in the pond. A tiny snake hid
under a maple leaf. Chen sat on the lawn and
drew for hours.

Soon Chen's room looked quite different. His
zoo pictures still hung on the walls. But so did
paintings of turtles, snakes, and other animals he
found in his yard.

Mom and Dad came in to admire his art. "I
still miss my old zoo," Chen sighed. "But I'm glad
I discovered the zoo in our back yard!"

Comprehension Check

Summarize

Read "A Challenge for Chen" again.
Then summarize the story.

Think About It

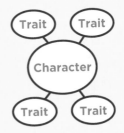

1. Why doesn't Chen want to
   move? Use details from the
   story to fill in the chart.
2. Why is it important to be
   flexible in new situations?
3. Think about a big change you have
   experienced. What did you gain because
   of this change?
4. Aside from the animals, what parts of Chen's
   new paintings will be different?

Write About It

If you were Chen's friend, what would you
suggest as a new idea or theme for his
paintings? Write about the advice you would
give Chen.

Skills and Strategies

Decoding

Decode these words. What do you notice about the spellings?

solar	other	flavor	polar
singer	under	collar	honor
actor	winter	razor	sugar

Vocabulary

beggars   explorers   helicopters

protectors

Comprehension

CAUSE AND EFFECT A cause is something that makes an action happen. The action that happens as a result of the cause is the effect.

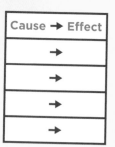

A Cause and Effect Diagram helps you ask questions to figure out what happens in a story (an effect) and why it happens (a cause).

Find the causes and effects.

Horses and Their Protectors

There are wide open spaces in the West. You can watch wild horses roam. Each space is a sanctuary, or safe place, for wild horses.

These wild horses are descendants of horses that came here with explorers. They ran wild for years. When food was scarce, they wandered into cities. People gathered them with helicopters, and became their protectors.

These wild horses sometimes act like beggars when they see food. But feeding them is not allowed. They can find the food they need themselves.

Make a **Cause and Effect Diagram** for "Horses and Their Protectors." Use it to help you find the causes and effects in the passage.

WILD HORSES OF THE WEST

by Toby Taylor

LIVING UNDER THE STARS

Horses live all around us. Kids and grownups can ride horses at a stable. Some horses are capable of helping city police officers. These horses live in barns and are cared for by their owners.

Other horses live in the wild and do not belong to anyone. These horses run free and eat grass and wild plants. They do not live in barns, and they sleep under the stars.

Most of these wild horses live in the West, on the Great Plains. They are descendants of horses that lived ages ago.

Those horses came here with explorers. People rode these horses to hunt and fight. Some of the horses ran off and joined other horses to form herds. These horses took care of each other and ran free in the wild.

Wild horses on the open range in Wyoming

Today's wild horses live in herds, too. Each herd has an older male horse and a few female horses. The herd eats, sleeps, and runs together.

Sometimes a new male horse tries to enter a herd. The older male fights back. The horse who wins the fight becomes the herd's leader.

The older horse is usually able to win, and the younger horse leaves. A female horse might go with him. These horses will then start their own herd.

These wild stallions fight to be leader of the herd.

The lead female horse leads her herd to food and water. She also finds shelter during storms. The male horse stands at the edge of his herd and looks for danger.

For wild horses, danger takes many forms. Horses could be hurt by a tornado on the plains. Another horse or animal might try to harm the herd. Males need to beware of bobcats, bears, and hungry wolves.

But their biggest danger comes from people.

A stallion watches over his herd.

A wild horse in a Maryland State Park looks through a car window.

Many people like wild horses. Some even make trips to see wild horses.

People will follow a herd in a car or a bus. They might try to take pictures of a herd running on the Plains. There are photos of wild horses splashing in a river. But people must be careful, because cars and buses can hurt wild horses.

Most people enjoy seeing wild horses. But some people say wild horses cause problems.

WILD HORSES IN THE CITY

Farmers think wild horses are beggars. They say the horses eat their crops and grass. These farmers want to be able to sell more crops. They also want their own animals to eat the grass on the farm.

Other people say there are just too many wild horses. When there isn't much food, the wild horses trot into cities and towns. They begin eating grass and plants in parks or backyards.

These wild horses eat crops and grass.

A helicopter is used to round up wild horses in Nevada.

Many admire wild horses. No one wants to hurt them. They just want wild horses to stay out of cities and towns.

People try to force horses to leave. Helicopters are used to chase horses into a trap. Once caught, some of these horses are tamed and sold. They might be trained to ride with people or help farmers.

Some wild horses can't be sold because they are too old or because they cause problems. They go back to the wild.

But some wild horses are lucky, and they go to a sanctuary. People who like wild horses created places like this so that horses can roam free.

Wild horses run in herds at a sanctuary. Instead of being cared for, these horses act just like they would in the wild. Wild horses can eat and drink on land that protectors set aside. This keeps them safe and happy.

Wild horses run across a prairie on the Great Plains.

Wild horses run free on the plains.

Tame horses rest on a split rail fence on a Vermont farm.

Wild horses may look like their tame cousins, but they lead different lives. On the plains and in sanctuaries, wild horses run free in the sun and wind. Horses that live with people may not get to run quite as much. But these horses are loved and cared for. Free or tame, horses are special animals.

Comprehension Check

Summarize

Read "Wild Horses of the West" again. Then summarize the selection.

Think About It

1. What causes farmers to have problems with wild horses? Use details from the selection to fill in your chart.

Cause	➔	Effect
	➔	
	➔	
	➔	
	➔	

2. Why do people choose to help wild animals?

3. Imagine that you can set up a sanctuary for an animal. Which animal would you choose?

4. Reread p. 231 of "Humpback Whales." How are the dangers to humpback whales similar to the dangers to wild horses? Give details from both selections in your answer.

Write About It

Can you think of another safe way to keep wild horses out of farms and cities? Explain.

Skills and Strategies

Decoding

Decode these words. What do you notice about the spellings?

space	crack	favorite	handy
shaker	replace	castle	glancing
mistake	contact	draft	strayed

Vocabulary

description   mission   discussion

nation   wealthy

Comprehension

CAUSE AND EFFECT A cause is something that makes an action happen. The action that happens as a result of the cause is the effect.

Cause → Effect
→
→
→
→

A Cause and Effect Diagram helps you ask questions to figure out what happens in a story (an effect) and why it happens (a cause).

Read

Look for the causes and effects.

A Mission for Leaders

Sometimes a nation, state, or city becomes a popular place to live. A nation might find gold and become wealthy. The city, nation, or state must prepare for more people.

Dealing with this issue is a mission for leaders. The leaders meet to have a discussion and form a plan. They write descriptions of what they hope to do, and what they can really do.

This helps them to make nicer schools, smoother roads, greener parks, and other places people can enjoy!

Make a **Cause and Effect Diagram** for "A Mission for Leaders." Use it to help you find the causes and effects in the passage.

They Came to California

by Tracy Yang

In 1848, a man discovered gold in California. It made him rich. Other people wanted to find gold and get rich quickly. So they came to California from all over the world. This was the beginning of the Gold Rush.

Jack lived in California as the Gold Rush took place. He was ten years old. This is his description of the Gold Rush.

Jack's path to the Gold Rush

Jack's Travels

My name is Jack. My ma, my pa, and I came to California in 1849. That was three years ago. My parents had a dream. They wanted to find gold and be rich.

We left our house in Wisconsin in March of 1849. We rode all the way to California on mules. We were on a mission. We were not going to stop until we found gold.

It was a hard trip. The days were long and burning hot. Water was hard to find. We saw men on the road selling water. It cost as much as $100 for a single cup!

We met a lot of Native Americans on the way. Some of them helped us find roots and nuts to eat, and rivers to drink from. They became our protectors when we needed help.

Miners traveling in search of gold during the Gold Rush

Gold prospectors looking for gold at a mine in California

When we arrived in California, we were so happy. My pa felt hopeful. He was going to find gold. We were going to be rich!

Pa had a discussion with a man on the trail. He told Pa that gold was easy to find. It was easy to dig up because it was not deep in the ground. My pa got some tools. He left every day at sunrise to dig.

From Trail to Camp

We lived in a camp with many men. They were prospectors, too.

I was the only kid who lived in our camp. Most of the men had left their families at home.

My ma cooked for the miners. I helped her bake bread and cakes. I also ran everywhere. I felt like an explorer! I liked to see all the action as men dug for gold.

The Gold Hill mining camp in California

A ship sailing around Cape Horn on the way to the California Gold Rush

Travelers from all over the world came looking for gold. People came from China, from France, and even from Chile! All of them hoped that they would find gold.

Some of the people came in boats. It took them six months to get across the sea.

Other people walked or rode across the United States like we did. They did not have a lot of food or water on the trip.

Chinese workers panning for gold in California

Thousands of people were here. All of them had dreams. They wanted to have more gold than a king or queen.

The men spent the day digging for gold. They worked all day, and did not sleep or eat much. All of the men lived in small tents. I guess it wasn't much fun for them.

My pa never struck gold. He worked hard. My ma worked hard too. But we never got rich.

My pa stopped looking for gold after a year. He started a boarding house for miners in June 1851. Now I help him and Ma with the business.

I like it here. I liked seeing all the men dig for gold. I like being with my ma and pa. I'm glad that I live in California.

Miners stayed in boarding houses during the California Gold Rush.

The Gold Rush made some people wealthy. But most of the people who went to California found no gold. They did not get rich, but many stayed in California. They set up shops and hotels. This place became their home.

The Gold Rush brought a lot of people to California. It also made California a rich place. It helped America grow and become the nation it is today.

This map provides a good picture of the San Francisco area during the Gold Rush.

THE CITY OF SAN FRANCISCO.
BIRDS EYE VIEW FROM THE BAY LOOKING SOUTH-WEST.

Comprehension Check

Summarize

Read "They Came to California" again. Then summarize the story.

Think About It

1. What happened when gold was found in California? Use details from the story to fill in the chart.

2. How would Jack's life be different if his family had not come to California?

Cause → Effect
→
→
→
→

3. If a Gold Rush happened today, and you lived far away, would you go? Explain.

4. How do you think the Gold Rush experience might have differed for American miners, and miners from other countries?

Write About It

Do you think that the miners who found gold lived happily ever after? Why or why not?

Skills and Strategies

Decoding

Decode these words. What do you notice about the spellings?

timetable	timid	animal	kindly
mixture	slight	vine	cricket
rabbit	divide	picture	campfire

Vocabulary

situation	treasure	creature
shelter	guard	relaxed

Comprehension

THEME Theme is the overall idea the author wants to tell in a story. Learning the theme will help you understand the story.

A Theme Map can help you identify an author's theme.

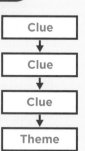

Try to figure out the theme.

A Wild Situation

Mike and Kim were in a tough situation. They had a treasure, but no place to keep it safe. At first, they fought over the treasure. They pulled it back and forth. Suddenly, they heard the growl of a wild creature. It was trying to take their treasure! Mike and Kim needed a plan.

Quickly, Mike and Kim set up a shelter together. They put the treasure inside. They took turns standing guard.

At last, their dog Trixy went upstairs, and Mike and Kim relaxed. They could eat their treasure in peace! The hot dogs tasted great!

Make a **Theme Map** for "A Wild Situation." Then use it to help you find the theme of the passage.

Fright
in the Forest

by Tanya Johnson
illustrated by Tim Egan

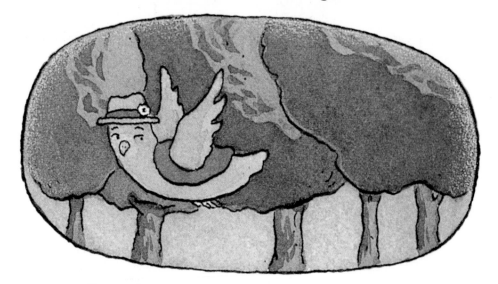

A Time for Discussion

The animals of Nature Forest spent most of their time alone. They ate, slept, relaxed, and even played by themselves. They did not visit each other or help each other. The animals were not friends.

One day, however, all of the animals came together for a meeting. They had to discuss an important situation. There was an odd mixture of sounds in the forest.

Owl led the meeting. He asked the animals to describe the odd noises they had been hearing.

Bear explained, "I hear a loud jingle. It sounds like a long chain being dragged. I do not like it."

"I hear thumping sounds. I am scared," added Deer.

"Screech, screech, screech – that is the sound I hear," described Rabbit. She was shaking with fear.

Raccoon had lived in Nature Forest longer than the other animals. He spoke next.

"These sounds remind me of a strange creature. The creature lived in Nature Forest a long time ago. No one ever met the creature. We just heard it. It would jingle, thump, and screech. It made noise all the time. We were scared. The creature made us unhappy."

Raccoon kept talking. "We learned before that we had to join together to stay safe. We have forgotten that lesson."

Owl nodded, and said, "The creature will not harm a large group of us. It will stay away if we stick together."

All the animals agreed with Raccoon and Owl. They needed to set up a safe place. Owl told the animals to meet at Picture Point. He told them to arrive that afternoon.

Life at Picture Point

All of the animals met at Picture Point that afternoon. The first thing they did was make a shelter. Beaver measured logs for the walls. Rabbit and Mouse picked up leaves for the top of the shelter. Raccoon was the guard.

The animals worked hard. They also worked together. The animals did not hear the creature at all as they set up the shelter.

Next, the animals began to look for food. Owl and Bird got nuts from a tree. Bear picked berries from a vine. Rabbit pulled leaves from bushes. A jumble of food was put in a basket. All of the food was in one place.

The animals helped each other find food. They did not hear a peep from the creature as they worked.

The animals prepared the food. Piles of fruit, chopped leaves, and sweets were set on the table. All of the animals sat down for a wonderful dinner.

The animals talked as they ate. Raccoon told jokes while Mouse giggled and squeaked. The animals did not hear the creature at all as they ate dinner.

After dinner, the bear cubs started a game. The animals played hide-and-seek and tag. Then they sang forest songs and danced. They were having way too much fun to be afraid.

The animals played games for a long time. They did not hear the creature at all as they played.

It had been a long day. The animals sat at a campfire and talked.

Owl began, "We had fun today. We talked, played, and worked together."

"We did not hear the creature at all," added Bear.

Raccoon spoke. "We are friends. Friends are a treasure. We need to be protectors for each other. Then the creature will never come back!"

All the animals in Nature Forest agreed. It was best to stick together. The animals stayed friends, and the creature did not come back!

Comprehension Check

Summarize

Read "Fright in the Forest" again. Then summarize the story.

Think About It

1. What did the animals in Nature Forest really learn? Use details from the story to fill in the chart.

2. What are the benefits of working and being friends with others?

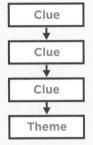

3. Describe a fear you have now, or had before. How did you deal with that fear?

4. Some birds live, eat, and fly in groups. Why would staying in a group be helpful for birds?

Write About It

Think of the last time you needed someone's help. What happened? How did they help you, and how did you feel?

Skills and Strategies

Decoding

Decode these words. What do you notice about the spellings?

shells	steal	speck	festival
medium	felt	complete	spend
copy	supreme	speak	blend

Vocabulary

remarkable	tortoise	span
marine	survive	

Comprehension

MAKE GENERALIZATIONS

Use what you know to decide if something is true for a group.

Information from Text	
Prior Knowledge	
Generalization	

A Generalization Chart helps you make statements that describe ideas or events.

Make a generalization about nature.

Exploring Nature

Many authors write about nature, and artists draw it. What is this remarkable thing that gets so much attention?

Nature is the living world around us. Plants, animals, land, sky, and water are all part of nature. Some animals, like the tortoise, live on land. Tortoises can have a long life span. Other creatures, like sea lions, live in the ocean. They are called marine animals.

There are many animals and plants in the world. They are all trying to grow and survive. Don't wait—go explore nature today!

Make a **Generalization Chart**. Read "Exploring Nature." Form a generalization for each paragraph before making one for the whole passage.

Galapagos:
Exploring a Dream

by Marcel Fitzway
illustrated by Howard S. Friedman

Feathers and Shells

In this big world of ours, there are many remarkable places to see. One such place is a chain of islands near South America. This place is called the Galapagos Islands. The islands are home to strange and amazing animals. These creatures can't be found anywhere else. People who study nature go to the Galapagos. They sometimes stay for years.

The Galapagos tortoise is the most famous creature on the islands. The islands were named after this large animal. It can weigh more than three people!

The tortoise grows a round and thick shell that keeps it safe. The shell's thickness makes it hard for hungry enemies to sink their teeth into them.

This tortoise has a long life span. It can live to be 150 years old!

The tortoise shares the land with other animals. The marine iguana is one of them. There are no other lizards that can swim in the sea like this iguana.

In the morning, this animal lies out on rocks or sand. This is a way for it to warm up its body. It dives deep into the sea to cool down when it gets too hot. The iguana also finds food in the sea.

Many rare birds live on the islands, too. They come in lots of sizes and colors. Many of them have strange traits.

The waved albatross can only be found on one of the islands, called Española. This huge bird has a wingspan of over eight feet. It weighs close to nine pounds.

A bird on the islands that does not fly is the Galapagos penguin. It might be strange to think that a penguin can live in a warm place. It works hard to keep cool. It holds its wings away from its body. This helps the heat leave its body faster. A penguin holds its wings over its feet to block the sun. The sun can burn its skin, just like the sun can burn us!

From Reef to Rocks

Visitors to the Galapagos Islands are fond of sea lions. These furry animals like to be a part of things. Their nosy nature makes them swim close to people in the sea.

When they are not swimming, sea lions often lie on rocks. They like being lazy, but their laziness could get them into trouble! Sea lions have to stay alert. They must look out for Galapagos sharks.

The Galapagos Islands are made up of layers of lava from underwater volcanoes. As the layers cooled, they formed the islands as they are today. It is strange to think that any animal can survive on such harsh land. A man named Charles Darwin found out why animals are able to stay there.

Darwin set off from England on a mission to study nature. He followed the creatures on the islands. He studied the plant life, too. He found that animals change their ways of life to keep on living.

The Galapagos Islands is one of the most unspoiled places on Earth. But early sailors who visited the islands upset the natural balance. They brought with them animals that were not native to the area.

Now, people understand the importance of keeping these islands as they are. Visitors must always keep the rules in mind. A major rule is that people must not touch or take things. It doesn't matter whether it is a small shell or a large animal.

Nature lovers want to see how animals act in the wild. These islands are a treasure that makes such dreams come true.

Comprehension Check

Summarize

Read "Galapagos: Exploring a Dream" again.
Then summarize the selection.

Think About It

1. Were you surprised to
   learn that penguins live in
   the Galapagos? Use details
   to fill in the chart.

Information from Text	
Prior Knowledge	
Generalization	

2. Why is it important to protect the Galapagos?

3. Describe a place that you think is unique.

4. Reread p. 280 of "The Edge of the World!"
   How was Robert Peary's experience similar
   to that of Charles Darwin?

Write About It

The Galapagos tortoise can live to be over 150
years old. What do you think the world will be
like in 150 years?

Skills and Strategies

Decoding

Decode these words. What do you notice about the spellings?

goal	possible	total	flock
topic	coastal	crop	hopeful
roadrunner	probably	postage	popular

Vocabulary

gliders	relying	controls
coast	income	

Comprehension

AUTHOR'S PERSPECTIVE It is important to know how an author feels about a topic. What is the author's point of view towards the subject matter?

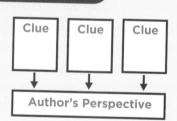

An Author's Perspective Map can help you understand the author's perspective.

Try to figure out the author's perspective.

Flying Free

Think how free a flying bird must feel! People thought about this for a long time. That is why there are things like planes and hang gliders. Hang gliders look like large kites. They come in many colors.

Hang gliding relies on the wind. It is the closest thing to really flying! But it is not easy. People must take classes to learn to use a hang glider's controls. Then flying on a windy coast is fun.

People who teach flying are usually paid well. They earn a high income. It is a great way to have fun and live well!

Make an **Author's Perspective Map** for "Flying Free." Fill in the clues that tell about author's perspective. Then use the clues to retell the passage.

Wilbur and Orville Wright
Heroes of Flight

by Renee Barry
illustrated by Dick Smolinski

Flight Long Ago

Airplanes are a big part of our lives today. They can take us just about anywhere in the world in a short time. This helps business people do their jobs.

Over a hundred years ago, people only dreamed about flying. Wilbur and Orville Wright changed all that in 1903. They flew in an airplane that they had made after years of hard work.

Wilbur and Orville Wright did not invent the airplane. Men made gliders and large kites years before the Wright brothers' flight. But the kites had no pilots, and the gliders had no controls. The Wright brothers made the first airplane that could be controlled in the air.

The Wright brothers got interested in flight when they were just boys. In 1878, Wilbur was 12 and Orville was 8 years old. Their father gave them a toy helicopter. This toy could really fly! Wilbur and Orville loved it, and wanted to make their own flying machine.

That year, the boys started making and flying little machines. Wilbur and Orville were very close and did a lot of things together. They made a good team.

When Wilbur and Orville grew up, they did not stop thinking about flying. Flying was not a job then, so they set up a printing shop. This situation gave them the income to make flying machines when they had free time.

Then the brothers got interested in bikes. In the 1890s, they had their own shop where they made bikes. Even at the bike shop, they studied flying and machines. Wilbur and Orville still dreamed of flying.

Reaching the Goal of Flight

Wilbur and Orville noticed that most new flying machines had no controls. The Wrights used what they knew about bikes to try to fix the problem. They looked at books about flying machines. They also studied birds in flight to get ideas. The Wrights even found a way to make the plane's wings tilt left or right.

First Wilbur and Orville tried their plan with a huge kite. Then they made gliders. They made test flights at Kitty Hawk, North Carolina in 1900 and 1901.

Kitty Hawk was a fine place to fly because it was on the Atlantic coast. There, the swiftness of the winds helped lift those gliders. Despite this, the gliders did not fly well. The Wrights could not control them well or get them to rise high enough.

The Wrights did not give up hope. They built a wind tunnel to test wing shapes and wing spans. At last they made a plane that had controls.

Next, they made an engine to give the plane power to fly without relying on wind. Then they added propellers. This was something that no one had tried before.

By the winter of 1903, the airplane was finished. The Wrights had to wait to fly because of bad weather.

At last, on December 17, 1903, the Wrights flew their plane. It rose off the ground and made several flights. The longest was 852 feet.

The Wright brothers had truly reached their goal. They had invented an airplane that could be controlled in the air. They did not stop with this first plane. They kept making better airplanes and airplane parts.

Over time, planes got larger in size. People started making them out of metal and rubber instead of wood. Engines got stronger, and planes flew longer distances.

Today's planes don't look much like Orville and Wilbur Wright's plane. That flight at Kitty Hawk was just the first step on the road to flying. Orville and Wilbur Wright simply got a remarkable idea off the ground.

Comprehension Check

Summarize

Read "Wilbur and Orville Wright: Heroes of Flight" again. Then summarize the selection.

Think About It

1. What does the author want you to know about the Wright brothers? Use details from the selection to fill in the chart.

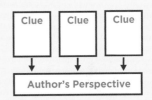

2. Why are experiments and inventions important to the world?

3. Can you imagine a machine you could build to make people's lives easier? Describe your machine.

4. How would the world be different without airplanes? Explain.

Write About It

Pretend you have an airplane ticket to any city in the world. Where would you go?

Skills and Strategies

Decoding

Decode these words. What do you notice about the spellings?

understood	broom	toolshed	swoosh
foolishness	rookie	smooth	hooded
footstep	shampoo	cooking	harpoon

Vocabulary

underground	scent	communicate
cocoon	colonies	

Comprehension

DESCRIPTION An author picks words carefully to paint a picture. Description words often have to do with the five senses: seeing, hearing, tasting, touching, and smelling.

Using a Description Web will help you to list details about something in a story.

Find the description words.

Ants and Termites

Ants and termites are good for the rain forest. Many live underground. Both have a special way to communicate. They can use scent to send messages.

Termites nest in large colonies. There is much to do. They split the work.

The queen lays large piles of eggs. When a little bug wriggles out of an egg, it is called a larva. It looks like a tiny worm.

While the ant larva makes a cocoon, the termite does not. But these bugs do have a lot in common. They both get the job done!

Make a **Description Web** for "Ants and Termites." Then use it to write about the passage.

ZOOM IN ON ANTS!

by Trent Locker

Ants Are Everywhere You Look

Everywhere you look, you can find ants. Go on a picnic and you will see ants stealing food. Look at the sidewalk while taking a walk. You may see ants crawling between the cracks. Smell a flower and you might see an ant on the leaf.

You can find ants inside, too. Ants might make a home in your kitchen. They like sugar and sweet food.

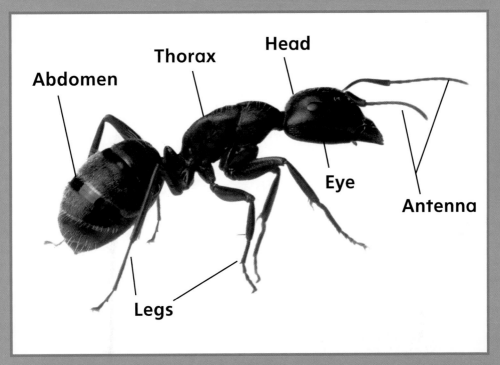

Abdomen Thorax Head Eye Antenna Legs

An ant's body

Ants are insects. Every insect has a body with three parts. Like all insects, ants have six legs. These legs grow from the middle section.

Ants have two eyes. Each is made up of many smaller eyes. These eyes give ants a good picture of the world. An ant also has two antennae on its head. They control how ants feel and smell things. These features help ants survive.

Some female ants lay eggs. First, the female makes a hole in the ground. She rests in the hole all winter. In spring, she lays her eggs. Worker ants feed the eggs as they grow.

The eggs go through several stages as they grow. In the last stage, the ant stays inside a cocoon, a silky case. After about eight weeks, the adult ant comes out.

Ants carrying eggs

An ant hill

There are about 8000 different kinds of ants in the world. An ant can be as tiny as a dot. It can also be over one inch long. That's big for an ant!

An ant does not live by itself. Ants live in groups called colonies. Small colonies have just a few ants in them. Large colonies might have millions of ants. They live and work together in a nest with many rooms.

Taking Good Care of Each Other

When people live and work together, they all rely on each other. Ants are like that, too.

Two ant jobs are queen and worker. Queen ants lay eggs. Worker ants look after a queen and her eggs. They also take good care of the ant nest. They help gather food, too. Worker ants come in different sizes. Big and little worker ants help each other.

Ants work together to carry a pine needle.

A wood ant carries a larva, an immature ant.

Ants eat many kinds of food. Ants might eat insects or insect eggs. Ants might also eat tree sap. Some ants eat other ants.

Ants can grow their own food. They gather parts of plants and insects. They bring these things back to their nest. They use them to feed a fungus, or mold, that grows in the nest. The fungus grows like a garden. When it is grown, the ants will eat it.

Leaf cutter ants are a type of ant that grows a fungus garden. They eat fungus because they cannnot eat plants.

The ants use their sharp jaws to cut leaves from plants. They travel in long lines far into the forest, in search of leaves. Then they carry the leaf pieces back to their nests.

These ants live in rain forests, in giant underground colonies. Three to eight million ants live in one colony.

Leaf cutter ants on a branch

Ants cannot talk on a telephone, but they have a special way to communicate. When worker ants find food outside the nest, they carry it home. They leave a scent on the trail. Then, more worker ants follow the trail so they can collect the food.

Ants send out a smell when they are in danger, too. When other ants smell it, they come to help the ants in danger.

African army ants on the march

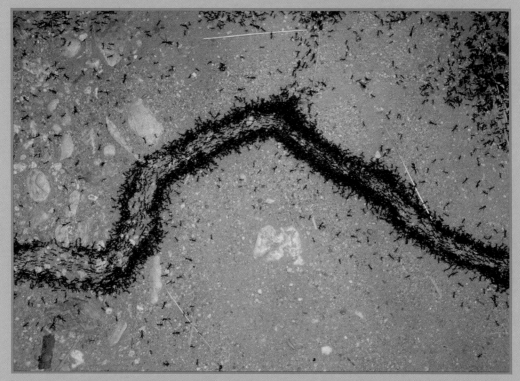

A child watching ants in an exhibit

When you think of ants, you might think of how they spoil picnics. But ants do good things, too.

Ants eat insects that can be harmful. Ants also help make soil richer. They dig up the dirt to make their nests. When ants gather seeds for nests, they drop some of them. Then new plants can grow.

Ants might bother us at times, but they are very important to our world!

Comprehension Check

Summarize

Read "Zoom in on Ants!" again. Then summarize the selection.

Think About It

1. Pick a passage from the selection that you think is a description. Use details to fill in the chart.

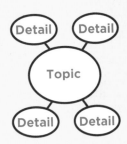

2. Why is it important for creatures to communicate?
3. Many people think insects are pests. Could you explain to someone how insects can be good?
4. What other creatures do you know that work together in a large group? How are they similar to the ant?

Write About It

Many people have jobs where they have to work together. Describe a project that required you to work with others.

Skills and Strategies

TITLE	DECODING	VOCABULARY	COMPREHENSION
Unit 1 pages 6–65			
6 Miss Tan's Hints	/a/a pack, /e/e set, /i/i spill, /o/o stop, /u/u mud	hint, news, odd, gym, hunt	Make Inferences and Analyze: Problem and Solution
18 In the Hot Sand	/a/a pack, /e/e set, /i/i spill, /o/o stop, /u/u mud	desert, cactus, tunnels, dusk, shimmer	Summarize: Main Idea and Details
30 Where Should We Go?	/ph/ph phone, /sh/sh brush, /th/th with, /hw/ wh when	national, trek, raft, fond, canyons	Summarize: Main Idea and Details
42 Kate in Space	/ā/a_e same, /ē/e_e these, /ī/i_e like	vanished, relate, chamber, bases, pit	Make Inferences and Analyze: Character
54 At Home with Whales	/ō/o_e stove, /ū/u_e tune	peered, pride, dove, fins, overflowing, locate	Make Inferences and Analyze: Character, Setting, Plot
Unit 2 pages 66–125			
66 Gail At the Game	/ā/ay stay, ai main	arranged, secured, rude, fame, spite	Make Inferences and Analyze: Author's Purpose
78 A Year in My Life	/ē/e she, ee seem, ea dream, y happy	feast, frame, gulf, cheap, steamboat	Generate Questions: Make Inferences
90 Up in the Sky	/ī/i quiet, y try, igh sight	dazzling, protected, soar, various, eager, festival	Make Inferences and Analyze: Fact and Opinion
102 Edison Shows the Way	/ō/o focus, oa boat, ow own	experiments, improve, invention, operated, provided	Generate Questions: Problem and Solution
114 The Snake Watcher	/ch/ch which, tch patch	rattle, clutched, nervous, poison, escape	Generate Questions: Make Inferences
Unit 3 pages 126–185			
126 Spring and the Beanstalk	/spr/spr spring, /skr/scr scream, /str/str stretch, /spl/spl splash	strolled, strained, scruffy, thunderstorm, sprinted	Evaluate: Author's Purpose
138 César Chávez: Righting a Wrong	/n/kn know, /r/wr write, /m/mb lamb, /t/bt debt	debt, roamed, attend, permanent, conditions, allow	Evaluate: Author's Purpose
150 Hard-Working Kids	/är/ar start	activities, completed, advisers, duty, theater, accepted	Summarize: Compare and Contrast
162 A Nation is Born	/ôr/or for, ore store	distressed, starving, fetch, rich, staff, declared	Summarize: Identify Sequence of Events
174 Storm Chasers	/ûr/er infer, ir first	anxious, increased, observing, equipment, occur, method	Evaluate: Summarize

366

ACKNOWLEDGMENTS

ILLUSTRATIONS
7-16: K. Michael Crawford. 43-52: Tom Leonard. 55-64: Lina Chesak. 67-76: Dom Lee. 79-88: John Trotta. 103-112: Steve Cieslawski. 115-124: Laura Bryant. 127-136: Selina Alko. 163-172: Constance Bergum. 187-196: Stephanie Milanowski. 199-208: Amy Tucker. 223-232 Nancy King. 247-256: Cynthia McGrellis. 259-268: Ralph Canaday. 283-292: Yangsook Choi. 319-328: Tim Egan. 331-340: Howard S. Friedman. 343-352 Dick Smolinski.

PHOTOGRAPHY
All photographs are by Macmillan/McGraw-Hill (MMH) except as noted below:

3: (tr) Ryan McVay/Getty Images; (br) PAUL & JOYCE BERQUIST/Animals Animals; 4: Ingram Publishing/Alamy; 5: Royalty-Free/CORBIS; 19: George H. H. Huey/CORBIS; 20: Kennan Ward/CORBIS; 21: George H. H. Huey/CORBIS; 22: (tr) PAUL & JOYCE BERQUIST/Animals Animals; (b) age fotostock/SuperStock; 23: David Muench/CORBIS; 24: Jonathan Nourok/Photo Edit; 25: (c) Claude Steelman/Wildshots; (b) John Cancalosi/Peter Arnold, Inc.; 26: Jess Lee Photography; 27: John Cancalosi/Peter Arnold, Inc.; 28: (t) Superstock, Inc./SuperStock; (inset) Barry Mansell/Naturepl.com; 31: Dynamic Graphics Group/Creatas/Alamy; 32-33: Angelo Cavalli/Index Stock Imagery; (bkgd) Siede Preis/Getty Images; 33: (b) Photodisc/Punchstock; 34: (tr) Getty Images; (b) Dynamic Graphics Group/Creatas/Alamy; 35: (t) SuperStock, Inc./SuperStock; (bkgd) Siede Preis/Getty Images; 36: (bc) Wetzel and Company; 36-37: (bkgd) Siede Preis/Getty Images; 37: (tc) C Squared Studios/Getty Images; (br) C Squared Studios/Getty Images; 38: (t) Tony Freeman/Photo Edit; 38-39: (bkgd) Siede Preis/Getty Images; 39: (b) Tom Bean/Getty Images; 40: © Troy and Mary Parlee/Magnum Photos; 91: Esbin-Anderson/AGEfotostock; 92: Esbin-Anderson/AGEfotostock; 93: SSPL/The Image Works; 94: (inset) Mary Evans Picture Library/The Image Works; 94-95: Peter Fakler/Alamy; 96: Jack Fields/CORBIS; 97: Michael Stone/Alamy; 98: Chris McGrath/Getty Images; 99: Mike Stone/Alamy; 100: China Photos/Getty Images; 103: Royalty-Free/CORBIS; 105: CORBIS; 110: Bettmann/CORBIS; 111: North Wind Picture Archives; 112: Bettmann/CORBIS; 139: Michael Rougier/Time Life Pictures/Getty Images; 140: © J. R. Eyerman/Time Life Pictures/Getty Images; 141: The Granger Collection, New York; 142-143: (t) Michael Rougier/Time Life Pictures/Getty Images; 143: The Granger Collection, New York; 144: Michael Rougier/Time Life Pictures/Getty Images; 145: 1976 George Ballis/Take Stock; 146-147: (b) Bettmann/CORBIS; 147: Paul Fusco/Magnum Photos; 148: Bettmann/CORBIS; 152: © Brand X Pictures/Alamy; 154: Figurine of a girl running, (bronze), Greek, (6th century BC)/British Museum, London, UK/ Bridgeman Art Library; 155: © Davis Barber/Photo Edit; 156: Bettmann/CORBIS; 157: CORBIS; 158: (tl) CORBIS; (c) Minnesota Historical Society/CORBIS; 159: Ingram Publishing/Alamy; 160: Michael Newman/Photo Edit; 175: Jim Reed/Photo Researchers, Inc.; 176: Jim Reed/Photo Researchers, Inc.; 177: Steve Bloom/Getty Images; 178: Jim Reed/CORBIS; 178-179: NOVASTOCK/Photo Edit; 180: Dennis MacDonald/Photo Edit; 181: A. T. Willett/Alamy; 182: Jeri Gleiter/Getty Images; 183: Jeff Greenberg/Alamy; 184: Paul Nevin/photolibrary/PictureQuest; 211: Lester Lefkowitz/CORBIS; 212: Tim Wright/CORBIS; 213: (t) Royalty-Free/Corbis; (bl) Royalty-Free/Corbis; 214: Bettmann/CORBIS; 215: Royalty-Free/Corbis; 216: (b) SuperStock/Alamy; 216-217: Steve Bloom Images/Alamy; 218: Lester Lefkowitz/CORBIS; 219: Ariel Skelley/CORBIS; 220: Medioimages/Alamy; 235: Dave and Sigrun Tollerton/Alamy; 236-237: (t) Digital Vision/PunchStock; 237: (b) D. Nunuk/Photo Researchers Inc.; 238: Apex News and Pictures Agency/Alamy; 239: Tony Arruza/CORBIS; 240: Carolyn Galati/Visuals Unlimited; 241: ATTAR MAHER/CORBIS SYGMA; 242-243: (t) Stuart Westmorland/CORBIS; 243: (b) Dave and Sigrun Tollerton/Alamy; 244: Joel W. Rogers/CORBIS; 271: © Stapleton Collection/CORBIS; 272: Topham/The Image Works; 273: Bettmann/CORBIS; 274: Getty Images; 275: Hulton-Deutsch Collection/CORBIS; 276: Stapleton Collection/CORBIS; 276-277: Galen Rowell/CORBIS; 278: Bryan& Cherry Alexander Photography; 279: (c) POPPERFOTO/Alamy; 280: Getty Images; 295: Royalty-Free/Corbis; 296: Jon Arnold Images/Alamy; 297: Howie Garber/Getty Images; 298: Royalty-Free/CORBIS; 299: franzfoto.com/Alamy; 300: Jeff Greenberg/Alamy; 301: Steve Craft/Masterfile; 302: Justin Sullivan/Getty Images; 303: Jeff Vanuga/CORBIS; 304: (t) Tom Brakefield/zefa/CORBIS; (inset) Andre Jenny/Alamy; 307: (c) Underwood & Underwood/CORBIS; 308: © Bettmann/CORBIS; 310: Kean Collection/Getty Images; 311: HultonArchive/Illustrated London News/Getty Images; 312: Timothy H. O'Sullivan/Getty Images; 313: Rischgitz/Getty Images; 314: Hulton Archive/Getty Images; 315: Bettmann/CORBIS; 316: CORBIS; 331: Robert E. Barber/Alamy; 333: Robert E. Barber/Alamy; 334: Paul Franklin/Oxford Scientific/PictureQuest; 336: Michael J. Kronmal/Alamy; 337: BISSON BERNARD/CORBIS SYGMA; 340: Galen Rowell/Masterfile; 355: Bob Anderson/Masterfile; 356: Todd Bannor/Alamy; 356-364: (bkgd) Jules Frazier/Getty Images; 357: Bob Anderson/Masterfile; 358: WildPictures/Alamy; 359: Elaine Johnson/Alamy; 360: plainpicture/Alamy; 361: blickwinkel/Alamy; 362: Bryan Mullennix/Getty Images; 363: Sinclair Stammers/Photo Researchers, Inc.; 364: Chris Sattlberger/Photo Researchers, Inc.